Pies & Tarts

FOR ALL SEASONS

ANNIE RIGG

Photography by Nassima Rothacker

quadrille

CONTENTS

Recipe note

Ingredients are listed in UK metric, followed by US cup/imperial measurements. Please follow one system of measurement when making the recipes.

JUST ONE SLICE

The radio's on, the next hour is clear, and the kitchen is tidy. You put on an apron and start rubbing cool cubes of butter into flour in a mixing bowl, your mind drifting off as the mixture turns to crumbs between your fingertips. Rolling out the pastry, lining the tart tin, crimping the edges and leaving it to chill while you move on to the filling; then watching it turn golden in the oven and smelling the buttery pastry as it bakes... there's something uniquely soothing about making a pie.

Pies for little hands, pies for big appetites, delicate, decorated tartlets for fancy occasions, extravagant fruit-filled tarts and pies for Friday-night TV dinners; refined tarts that take advantage of the best seasonal produce and rustic tarts that can be cobbled together from what you have in your store cupboards.

There's a pie or a tart for everyone and every season.

And what holds it all together is pastry. Pastry has a bad reputation, some folks believing that they can't make it. But like most cooking, and baking in particular, you need to follow a few rules. I have clumsy hands that are more suited to digging the garden than delicate pastry work and yet I can make light, flaky pastry. In my opinion a homemade pie should include homemade pastry (unless we're talking filo pastry in which case I'm the first in the queue to buy it). I recommend using good metal tart and pie tins – the best your budget will allow. They will be less likely to buckle in the oven and, if looked after, will last years. My advice for making pastry without fear is on the next page.

This book is simply divided in two: sweet and savoury. The recipes range in size from delicate mini pies and tartlets that are just enough for a couple of mouthfuls, through pies that'll heartily serve one person, right up to large-scale centrepiece tarts to serve at a gathering.

Finally, what's in a name and when is a pie a tart, and a tart a pie?

A pie will often be baked in an oven-to-table dish rather than in metal bakeware, and will most likely be double crusted, in other words with a pastry top, sides and bottom. If it doesn't have a pastry top, then a pie will at least have some type of lid covering the filling. Lemon meringue pie and crumble-topped fruit pies are examples of this; however, pumpkin pie throws this theory out of the window. Hand pies, such as empanadas or pop tarts, are also in this club, but on the periphery.

A tart usually has a more delicate, buttery pastry bottom and sides with its filling open to the elements, and can be sweet or savoury. A tart is, however, rarely filled with meat and more likely to be an elegant affair. A galette is a simple tart that's free-styling; it's a little more rough around the edges and has done away with the need for fancy bakeware.

Like most things in life, there's no clear-cut rule and anyway, breaking the rules is always more fun. So arm yourself with a rolling pin, dust your hands with flour and embrace the deliciously wonderful (and sometimes confused) world of pies and tarts.

PASTRY 101

I'm a firm believer that anyone can make decent pastry but some simple rules should be followed to ensure best results. Most of the pastry recipes in this book are made by hand rather than in a food processor and I urge you to give it a go. It gives a better texture and saves on washing up. Start by finding a mixing bowl that you can easily get your hands into.

Always use good ingredients, unsalted butter and free-range eggs. Make sure your butter is fridge-cold unless otherwise instructed – for pâte sablée you will need room-temperature butter but this is an exception rather than the norm. All liquids should be cold and eggs at room temperature. If your hands are warm, run them and your wrists under cold water for 30 seconds or so to cool them down.

Work quickly and have all the ingredients prepared before starting. By working quickly you will avoid the butter warming up in your hands and becoming greasy. Making sure that your bowl and work surfaces are cool will help, too.

Chilling pastry after mixing and again after rolling (and in between rolls and folds for puff pastry) is a vital step as this will allow the gluten in the flour to relax, the fats to firm up and cool down, and will make the resulting pastry easy to roll and less inclined to shrink during baking. Once baked, a well-rested pastry will have a better texture and be less inclined to toughness. I often chill my pastry overnight. Hot-water crust pastry is the exception to this rule and should be used while still warm or at room temperature, to make shaping easy.

When rolling out pastry, dust the work surface and rolling pin with plain flour and roll in even, smooth movements. Turn the pastry around by a quarter turn every now and then and dust the surface with more flour as and when needed to prevent it sticking. When making larger pies, roll the pastry to the required shape and thickness, then roll it around the rolling pin and gently lower it into the tart tin, starting at one side and unrolling the pastry as you go across. Gently press the pastry into the corners and ridges and trim off any excess from the top using a knife or by pressing the pastry against the top of the tin.

Preheating the oven properly is a key step to avoid pastry shrinking – if the oven is not hot enough the pastry will melt rather than bake into a crisp shell.

I do not necessarily use non-stick tins but I do use good-quality ones and solid baking sheets that are less likely to buckle.

Some pastry shells need to be 'blind-baked' before filling. Cover the base and sides of the raw, chilled pastry case with foil, pressing it into the corners and ridges for a neat inside edge to the finished pie. Half-fill with baking rice or dried pulses – this will weigh the bottom of the tart down as it cooks. I prefer rice to baking beans as the rice nestles into corners, making a clean, sharp edge, with the added bonus that rice is cheaper than baking beans.

I sometimes use tart rings (individual and large sized) with straight edges as opposed to fluted tins, as they give a crisp, clean edge and straight sides to your tarts and

continued »

continued »

SWEET PASTRY

an almost professional finish. They need to sit on solid baking sheets covered with parchment for lining and cooking. And, as they have no bases, the rings are simply lifted off once the tarts are cooked. And also, as they have no bases, you'll never have that odd-sock situation when you have an assortment of tart tins with no matching bases. Individual or small rings are often sold in packs of 8 or 10 and are available in cookware shops or online.

I like generosity when baking and prefer tarts to be deep-filled, therefore all of the large tart tins and rings used in this book have a depth of 3.5–4cm [1½in].

The easiest way to remove a large cooked tart from a fluted tin is to sit the tin on an upturned can or large jar and allow the outside ring to drop down to the work surface. Carefully slide a palette knife in between the tin base and the underside of the tart and gently push the tart onto your serving plate.

A final note about gluten-free cooking: it has come a long way in recent years and although you can make your own flour blends for baking using a variety of ingredients such as rice flour, potato flour, cornflour and tapioca flour, you can now easily buy packs of blended, plain gluten-free flour. This is used in much the same way as regular flour but sometimes with the addition of a small amount of xanthan gum. Refer to packs for more detailed instructions. Gluten-free puff pastry is also now widely available in most supermarkets either as fresh or frozen.

I enjoy the rather gentle action of pastry making by hand. The end result will have a better texture than that made in a machine, with tiny nuggets of butter and liquid helping to create a more flaky pastry with a more delicate crumb.

Makes enough to line a 22–25-cm [8¾–10-in] tart or 6 deep fluted 10-cm [4-in] tart tins, or 12 muffin-tin size tarts

200g [1½ cups] plain [all-purpose] flour
a pinch of salt
125g [½ cup plus 1 Tbsp] unsalted butter, chilled and diced
40g [4½ Tbsp] icing [confectioners'] sugar, sifted
1 medium egg yolk
2 Tbsp ice-cold water
2 tsp lemon juice

Tip the flour and salt into a bowl. Add the butter and, using a round-bladed or palette knife, cut the butter into the flour until the pieces are half of their original size. Now switch to using your hands to rub the butter into the flour. Working quickly, pick up handfuls of the flour and butter and allow it to pass across your fingertips, gently pressing and rubbing the mixture as it falls back into the bowl. Still working quickly, continue rubbing the butter into the flour until there are only very small flecks of butter remaining.

Add the sugar and mix. Make a well in the middle of the mixture, add the egg yolk, ice-cold water and lemon juice and mix using the palette knife until the pastry starts to clump together. Gather into a ball using your hands and very lightly knead for 10 seconds until smooth. Flatten the pastry into a disc, wrap in cling film [plastic wrap] and chill for at least 2 hours.

PUFF PASTRY

If you only need half the quantity here to make any given pie I'd always recommend making this full quantity – it's tricky to make in smaller amounts and any unused will freeze brilliantly for use another time. Puff pastry is not that hard: you need to be methodical, neat and not rush any steps.

Makes about 650g [1lb 7oz], which is enough to make 2 Baked Tunworth (page 182), 4 Slow-Cooked Beef Short Rib & Mushroom Pies (page 165), 14 Apple & Marzipan Chaussons (page 66) or 1 large Quince Galette des Rois (page 134)

250g [1 cup plus 2 Tbsp] unsalted butter, chilled
150g [1 cup plus 2 Tbsp] plain [all-purpose] flour, plus extra for rolling out
100g [¾ cup minus ½ Tbsp] strong white flour
a pinch of salt
1 medium egg yolk
100–125ml [6–8 Tbsp] ice-cold water
1 tsp lemon juice

Dice 50g [3½ tablespoons] of the chilled butter. Combine both flours in a mixing bowl, add the salt and the diced butter and rub in using your fingers until the butter has been well incorporated into the flour.

Make a well in the middle of the dry ingredients, add the egg yolk, 100ml [6 tablespoons] ice-cold water and the lemon juice and mix using a round-bladed knife. Bring the dough together, adding up to 2 tablespoons more water if needed, but do not allow the dough to get too sticky. Gather the dough into a ball, flatten into a neat rectangle, cover with cling film [plastic wrap] and chill for 1 hour.

Lightly dust the work surface with plain flour and roll the dough out into a rectangle that is 3 times as long as it is wide and with one of the short sides closest to you. Place the remaining butter

between 2 sheets of baking parchment and use a rolling pin to flatten it into a neat square slightly smaller than one-third of the pastry rectangle. Place the butter on the middle third of the pastry rectangle and fold the bottom third up over it, brush off excess flour and fold the top third down so the butter is completely encased.

Turn the square 90° clockwise, dust the surface and rolling pin with more flour, and roll out the pastry again into a neat rectangle of similar size as before. Use short, sharp tapping and rolling actions rather than long sweeping rolls, and use your hands to try to keep the pastry as neat as possible as you roll it out. In the same way as you folded the dough before, fold the bottom third of the rectangle up over the middle third and the top third down, brushing off excess flour each time. Turn the square 90° clockwise, wrap in cling film and, keeping the square flat and in the same rotation, chill for 1 hour.

Dust the work surface with flour and roll the dough out again into the same-sized rectangle, keeping the sides and ends as neat as possible. Fold the dough up as before, turn the square 90° clockwise, and repeat this roll and fold. Cover with cling film, keeping the square in the same position, and chill again for another hour.

Repeat this rolling and folding a further 2 times, rolling the dough and folding in the same manner and turning it 90° clockwise between each fold. Chill again then roll the dough out one more time so that you have rolled the dough 6 times in total. Keep a note of the number of roll and folds that you do! Leave the pastry, covered and chilled, for at least 2 hours before using.

PATE SABLEE

Exceptionally, this pastry requires butter that is at room temperature, and is rich with egg yolks, vanilla and cream. It is an ideal pastry for delicate sweet tarts.

Makes enough to line a 20–22-cm [8–8¾-in] tart tin, or 6–8 individual 8–10-cm [3¼–4-in] tart rings or tins

100g [½ cup minus 1 Tbsp] unsalted butter, at room temperature
50g [5¾ Tbsp] icing [confectioners'] sugar
2 medium egg yolks
1 tsp vanilla extract
175g [1⅓ cups] plain [all-purpose] flour
a pinch of salt
1 Tbsp double [heavy] cream

Cream together the butter and icing sugar using a free-standing mixer fitted with the paddle or K-shaped attachment. When the mixture is pale and light – after a minute or so – add the egg yolks and vanilla extract and mix again until combined. Scrape down the sides of the bowl using a rubber spatula and add the flour, salt and ½ tablespoon of cream, and mix again until the dough starts to clump together – be careful not to overwork the dough, this is pastry not cake mix. Only add more cream if needed.

Tip the dough out onto the work surface and lightly knead to bring it together into a neat ball. Flatten into a disc, wrap in cling film [plastic wrap] and chill for at least 1 hour or until firm.

CREAM CHEESE PASTRY

This is one of the few pastry recipes in this book that makes use of the food processor. It can also be made by hand if you prefer but it is slightly stickier than other recipes.

Makes enough for 6 individual galettes, a 30-cm [12-in] galette, or a large double-crust pie to serve 6–8

150g [1 cup plus 2 Tbsp] plain [all-purpose] flour, plus extra for shaping
½ tsp baking powder
25g [2 Tbsp] caster [granulated] sugar
a pinch of salt
75g [⅓ cup] unsalted butter, chilled and diced
75g [⅓ cup] cream cheese, chilled
50g [½ cup] ground almonds
1 medium egg yolk
1 Tbsp cold milk or water

Tip the flour, baking powder, sugar and salt into the food processor bowl. Add the chilled, diced butter and use the pulse button until the mixture resembles fine sand and only small flecks of butter are still visible. Add the cream cheese in teaspoonfuls, with the ground almonds, egg yolk and milk and mix again until the dough starts to come together in large clumps.

Tip the dough out of the food processor onto the work surface and use lightly floured hands to bring the dough together into a neat ball, but do not overwork the pastry. Flatten into a disc, cover with cling film [plastic wrap] and chill for at least 2 hours before using.

SOURDOUGH PASTRY

If, like me, you make sourdough bread, you will be on the constant lookout for recipes to use up excess every time you refresh your starter. This recipe requires your starter to be active and at 100% hydration, i.e. fed an equal weight of flour to water and chilled before use.

Makes enough for a 22-cm [8¾-in] double-crust or latticed pie

175g [1⅓ cups] plain [all-purpose] flour
1 Tbsp caster [granulated] sugar
a good pinch of salt
150g [⅔ cup] unsalted butter, chilled and diced
175g [6¼oz] active starter, chilled (100% hydration)

Tip the flour into a bowl and add the sugar and salt. Add the chilled, diced butter and, using a palette or butter knife, cut the butter into the flour until the pieces are half their original size. Now switch to using your hands to rub the butter into the flour. Working quickly pick up handfuls of the flour and butter and allow it to pass across your fingertips, gently pressing and rubbing the mixture as it falls back into the bowl. Working quickly, continue rubbing the butter into the flour until there are only very small flecks of butter remaining.

Make a well in the middle of the ingredients, add the chilled sourdough and mix to combine, first using the knife and then your hands to gather the dough into a ball. Flatten into a disc, wrap in cling film [plastic wrap] and chill overnight until needed.

ROSEMARY & PARMESAN PASTRY

This is essentially a savoury shortcrust pastry with a few additions – a handful of grated Parmesan and some finely chopped herbs for a little extra jazz. You can play around with the herbs, adding thyme or oregano if that's your preference or what you have to hand.

Makes enough for a 20 x 30 x 4-cm [8 x 12 x 1½-in] tart or 40 mini tartlets

250g [1¾ cups plus 2 Tbsp] plain [all-purpose] flour
a good pinch each of salt and freshly ground black pepper
125g [½ cup plus 1 Tbsp] unsalted butter, chilled and diced
50g [¾ cup] finely grated Parmesan
1 Tbsp finely chopped rosemary
4 Tbsp ice-cold water
1 tsp cider vinegar or white wine vinegar

Tip the flour into a bowl and add the salt and black pepper. Add the chilled, diced butter and, using a round-bladed or palette knife, cut the butter into the flour until the pieces are half their original size. Now switch to using your hands to rub the butter into the flour. Working quickly, pick up handfuls of the flour and butter and allow it to pass across your fingertips, gently pressing and rubbing the mixture as it falls back into the bowl. Still working quickly, continue rubbing the butter into the flour until there are only very small flecks of butter remaining.

Add the Parmesan and rosemary and mix to combine. Make a well in the middle of the ingredients, add the ice-cold water and the vinegar and, using a palette knife, mix until the pastry starts to clump together. Gather into a neat ball, flatten into a disc, wrap in cling film [plastic wrap] and chill for at least 1 hour until needed.

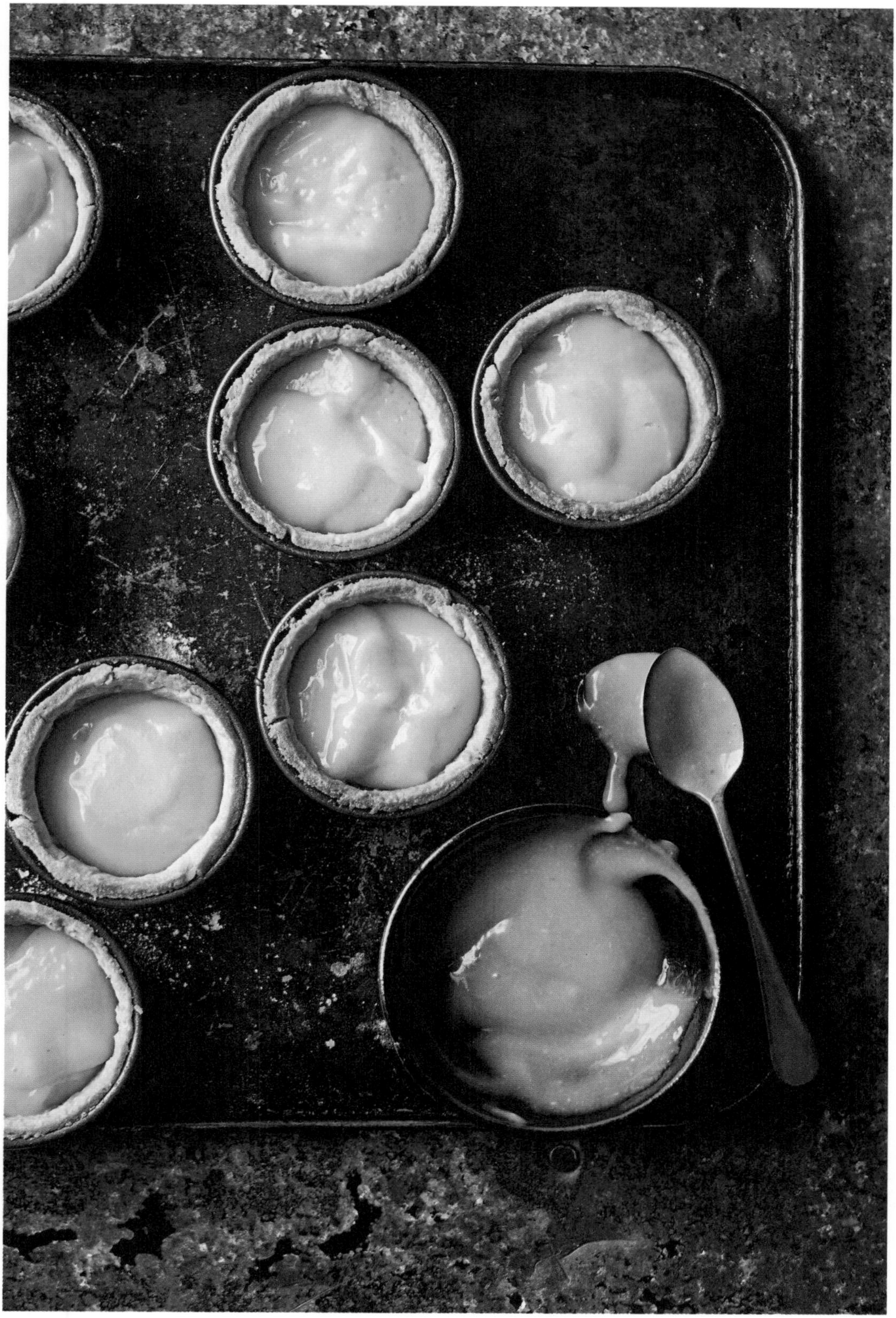

SWEET

MOCHA SFOGLIATELLE

I'm not going to lie – these shell-shaped, Italian pastries are a labour of love, but one that will leave you with an enormous sense of satisfaction and a kitchen full of delicious pastries. You'll need a pasta machine and a disposable piping bag.

Dough
425g [3¼ cups] plain [all-purpose] flour, plus extra for rolling out
3 Tbsp olive oil
175ml [¾ cup] cold water
a good pinch of sea salt
150g [⅔ cup] unsalted butter
125g [½ cup plus 1 Tbsp] lard

Filling
125ml [½ cup] milk
50ml [3½ Tbsp] water
100g [½ cup] caster [granulated] sugar
25g [¼ cup] cornflour [cornstarch]
2 medium eggs
a pinch of salt
50g [1¾oz] dark [bittersweet] chocolate (70% cocoa solids), chopped
1 tsp instant coffee dissolved in 1 tsp boiling water
125g [generous ½ cup] ricotta
icing [confectioners'] sugar, to serve

Makes 20

For the dough, sift the flour into a large mixing bowl and make a well in the middle. Add the olive oil, water and salt and mix until the mixture starts to clump together. Using your hands, bring the dough into a ball – do not be tempted to add more water – and knead for 2–3 minutes until smooth. Wrap the dough in cling film [plastic wrap] and chill for 1 hour.

Make the filling while the dough is resting. Heat the milk and water in a saucepan until just below boiling point. In a mixing bowl, whisk together the sugar, cornflour, eggs and salt. Pour the hot milk mixture into the bowl, whisk until smooth and return the mixture to the pan. Continue to cook over a low–medium heat until thickened, gently boiling and you can no longer taste the cornflour. Remove from the heat, pour into a bowl and add the chopped chocolate and coffee. Mix until smooth and the chocolate has melted, then add the ricotta and beat until smooth. Cover the surface with cling film [plastic wrap] and leave to cool then chill until needed.

Beat the butter and lard together until smooth then soften in the microwave until really soft and spreadable with a brush.

Position a pasta-rolling machine at one end of the work surface or kitchen table – you are going to need at least 1 metre [3 feet] of clear work surface.

Divide the dough into 6 evenly sized pieces, each weighing just over 100g [3½oz]. Roll one piece of dough into a rectangle roughly 5mm [¼in] thick and pass through the pasta machine on the widest setting. Fold the dough in half and pass through the machine again. Keep the work surface and the dough dusted with flour

continued »

continued »

to prevent sticking. Narrow the pasta rollers by one notch and pass the dough through again. Reduce the thickness of the rollers again and pass the dough through. Continue in this manner until you reach the thinnest setting – by now the dough should be as fine as silk and about 1 metre [3 feet] long.

Carefully, evenly and generously brush the entire surface of the dough strip with one-sixth of the super-soft butter and lard mixture. Trim the rounded ends from the pastry strip and, starting at one of the shorter ends roll the dough into a tight spiral log, gently pulling the dough towards you as you roll to keep the roll as tight as possible. Stop rolling when you get 2cm [¾in] from the end and set the roll to one side.

Roll another portion of dough out in the same manner as above, brush with the butter mixture, trim the ends and lay the first roll at one end so that the ends overlap by 1cm [⅜in]. Continue to roll the log so that you end up with a tight log roughly 10cm [4in] long and 4cm [1½in] wide. Wrap in cling film [plastic wrap] and place in the fridge. Repeat with the remaining pastry so that you have 3 neat rolls. Chill for 1 hour – not much longer or the butter will set too firm.

Preheat the oven to 200°C/400°F/Gas 6 and line 2 baking sheets with baking parchment. Scoop the mocha filling into a disposable piping bag and snip the end into a 1-cm [⅜-in] tip.

Taking one log at a time, cut into 1-cm [⅜-in] slices and, using your fingers, gently push the slice into a cone shape, similar in shape to an egg-cosy – be careful not to overly separate the pastry layers as you do so. You may find it easier to very lightly dust your fingers with flour. Fill the cone with a teaspoon of the mocha filling and press the ends together to seal. Repeat with the remaining pastry. Bake on the middle shelf of the oven for about 20 minutes until golden brown and crisp.

Transfer to a wire cooling rack and serve at room temperature, dusted with icing sugar.

ECCLES CAKES

You can of course use shop-bought puff pastry to make these traditional British pastries instead of your own flaky pastry; however, if you must, then it must be all-butter pastry. Mixed spice can be substituted for the allspice and nutmeg. While we're on the subject of twists and alternatives – why not fill the Eccles cakes with mincemeat and nuggets of marzipan?

Serve hot, warm or at room temperature, with either a mug of tea or with crumbly Lancashire cheese.

Flaky pastry
125g [¾ cup plus 2 Tbsp] strong white flour
125g [1 cup minus 1 Tbsp] plain [all-purpose] flour, plus extra for rolling out
a good pinch of salt
250g [1 cup plus 2 Tbsp] unsalted butter, chilled
about 125ml [½ cup] ice-cold water
1 tsp lemon juice

Filling
150g [generous 1 cup] currants
2 Tbsp Marsala
40g [3 Tbsp] unsalted butter
½ tsp freshly ground nutmeg
½ tsp ground allspice
1 tsp finely grated orange zest
1 tsp finely grated lemon zest
40g [3¼ Tbsp] soft light brown sugar
50g [1¾oz] candied peel
a pinch of salt

To glaze
1 medium egg white
3 Tbsp demerara [turbinado] sugar

You will need a 10–11-cm [4–4½-in] plain round cutter

Makes 12–14

To make the flaky pastry, combine both flours and the salt in a large mixing bowl. Cut the very cold butter into 2-cm [¾-in] dice and add to the flour. Cut the butter into the flour using a palette knife until the butter pieces are half their original size.

Sprinkle 125ml [½ cup] of water and the lemon juice over the mixture and mix to combine using the palette knife – add a little more water if needed to bring the dough together. It should be very raggedy with large pieces of butter still visible at this stage. Gently gather the dough into a ball, flatten into a disc and roll into a neat rectangle three times as long as it is wide – roughly 45 x 15cm [18 x 6in]. Roll the dough using a sharp tapping motion with the rolling pin rather than rolling back and forwards, and try to keep the sides and ends as neat as possible. Lightly dust the top of the dough with flour and fold the bottom third of the rectangle up into the middle third to cover and the top third down to cover that. You should end up with a neat, 3-layered pastry square. Cover with cling film [plastic wrap] or pop into a freezer bag and chill for at least 1 hour.

Lightly dust the work surface with flour and roll out the dough again into a 45 x 15-cm [18 x 6-in] rectangle, keeping the sides and ends as neat as possible. Fold the bottom third up into the middle and the top third back down on top. Turn the dough square 90° and repeat this rolling and folding another time. Cover the pastry and chill again for another hour.

continued »

continued »

While the dough is resting, prepare
the filling. Tip the currants into a small
saucepan, add the Marsala, butter, spices,
orange and lemon zests and sugar. Heat
gently over a low heat to melt the butter.
Mix well to combine, remove from the
heat, add the candied peel and leave to
cool and to allow the currants to soak up
the Marsala.

Roll the dough out on a lightly floured
surface to a thickness of 2–3mm [^{1}/$_{16}$–^{1}/$_8$in]
and, using the cutter, stamp out as many
rounds as you can. Neatly stack the scraps
and off-cuts together and roll and stamp
out again.

Lay the pastry rounds on the work surface
and spoon the currant mixture into the
middle of each, leaving a 1–2-cm [^{3}/$_8$–^{3}/$_4$-in]
border around the edges. Pull and fold the
pastry edges over the currants so that the
fruit mixture is encased in pastry. Flip the
Eccles cakes over and lightly roll out again
to about half the thickness. Arrange on a
baking sheet lined with baking parchment
and chill while you preheat the oven to
180°C/350°F/Gas 4.

Snip or cut 3 slashes into the top of each
pastry. Lightly beat the egg white until
frothy, brush over the top of the Eccles
cakes, sprinkle with the demerara sugar
and bake for 20 minutes until the pastry
is crisp and golden brown.

SWEET

22

MALTED CUSTARD TARTLETS
WITH BOURBON-SOAKED RAISINS

These little tarts pack a warm, boozy hit from the bourbon-soaked raisins that are lurking underneath a rich and creamy malted custard. Look out for bourbon with a rounded, warm flavour such as Maker's Mark. Barley malt extract is easily found in health food stores or online and has a flavour that cannot be substituted for anything else. These tarts are best served an hour or so after baking, when they are still slightly warm and the pastry is crumbly.

Soaked raisins
75g [about ½ cup] raisins
3 Tbsp bourbon
1 small cinnamon stick

Sweet pastry
200g [1½ cups] plain [all-purpose] flour, plus extra for rolling out
a good pinch of salt
125g [½ cup plus 1 Tbsp] unsalted butter, chilled and diced
40g [4½ Tbsp] icing [confectioners'] sugar
1 medium egg yolk
2 Tbsp ice-cold water
2 tsp lemon juice

Custard
4 large egg yolks
30g [2½ Tbsp] light muscovado sugar
10g [2 tsp] caster [granulated] sugar
½ tsp vanilla bean paste
2 Tbsp barley malt extract
a pinch of smoked sea salt flakes
200ml [generous ¾ cup] double [heavy] cream
100ml [⅓ cup plus 1 Tbsp] whole milk
a good grating of fresh nutmeg

You will need a 10–11-cm [4–4¼-in] plain round cutter and a 12-hole muffin tin

Makes 12

Start by tipping the raisins into a small saucepan. Add the bourbon and cinnamon stick and set the pan over a low heat to gently warm the bourbon without boiling. Remove from the heat, stir well and set aside for a good couple of hours or, better still, overnight, to allow the raisins to soak up all of the alcohol.

Make the sweet pastry following the instructions on page 11 and chill for at least 2 hours until firm.

While the pastry is chilling, prepare the custard. Drop the egg yolks into a mixing bowl and add both sugars, whisk to combine and add the vanilla bean paste, barley malt extract and the salt flakes. Gently whisk again until smooth. Measure the cream and milk into a small pan and heat until the surface of the liquid is shimmering and just below boiling point. Pour the hot milk and cream onto the egg and sugar mixture, whisking constantly until thoroughly combined. Try not to incorporate too much air into the custard – you want it to be silky smooth rather than foamy and full of bubbles. Strain the custard through a fine-mesh sieve into a jug and leave to cool to room temperature. Cover and set aside until all of the bubbles have burst on the surface of the custard.

SWEET

24

continued »

Roll the pastry out on a lightly floured
surface to a thickness of no more than
2mm [¹/₁₆in]. Using the round cutter, stamp
out as many rounds as you can from the
pastry, re-rolling the scraps and off-cuts
to stamp out more rounds – you will need
12 in total. Gently push the pastry into the
cups of the muffin tin to line smoothly, but
being careful not to stretch the pastry as
you do so. Chill the pastry cases for 20–30
minutes while you preheat the oven to
170°C/330°F/Gas 3½.

Prick the base of each pastry case, line
with a square of scrunched up foil and
fill with baking rice. Bake the pastry
on the middle shelf of the oven for about
20 minutes until pale golden. Remove
the foil and rice and return the pastry
to the oven for a further minute to dry
out the bases.

Divide the boozy raisins between the
pastry cases (discard the cinnamon) and
carefully pour the custard on top, being
careful not to spill any over the edges
of the pastry. Sprinkle the finely grated
nutmeg over the top and return the tarts to
the oven for a further 20 minutes until the
custard has just set.

Leave the tarts to cool in the tins for at
least 20 minutes then remove from the tins
and leave to cool on a wire rack. Serve just
warm or at room temperature.

PEANUT BUTTER & RASPBERRY LINZER TARTLETS

These little tartlets are a cross between a peanut butter cookie and a jam tart. I had imagined that this recipe would be perfect to make with – and for – children, but it seems that they have become rather popular in our grown-up peanut butter-loving house.

I like the combination of raspberry jam with peanut butter, but if you prefer strawberry or another flavour then feel free to use that.

125g [generous ½ cup] crunchy peanut butter (nothing worthy or fancy)
100g [½ cup minus 1 Tbsp] unsalted butter, at room temperature
50g [¼ cup] soft light brown sugar
25g [2¾ Tbsp] icing [confectioners'] sugar, plus extra for dusting
1 medium egg, lightly beaten
1 tsp vanilla extract
1 tsp lemon juice
225g [1¾ cups] plain [all-purpose] flour, plus extra for rolling out
¼ tsp baking powder
a pinch of salt
300g [10½oz] raspberry jam

You will need 2 x 12-hole muffin tins, a 6.5–7-cm [2½–2¾-in] fluted round cutter and a 3.5-cm [1¼-in] star-shaped cutter

Makes 18

Spoon the peanut butter into a bowl, add the softened butter and both sugars, and cream for a couple of minutes until soft and light. This is easiest with a free-standing mixer fitted with the K-shaped attachment, but is hardly taxing using a bowl, spatula and muscle power.

Add the beaten egg, vanilla and lemon juice and beat to combine. Sift the flour, baking powder and salt into the bowl and mix again until thoroughly combined. Bring the dough into a neat ball using your hands, flatten into a disc, cover with cling film [plastic wrap] and leave to rest at cool room temperature for 1 hour.

Preheat the oven to 180°C/350°F/Gas 4 and line the muffin tins with 18 paper cases.

Dust the work surface with flour and roll out the dough to a thickness of 3–4mm [⅛in] and, using the fluted round cutter, stamp out as many rounds as you can from the dough. Stamp out stars from the off-cuts in between the rounds. Gently press the round shapes into the paper cases so that they form shallow tarts. Gather any dough off-cuts into a ball and re-roll and stamp out more rounds and stars.

Spoon 1 rounded teaspoon of jam into each tart and top with a pastry star. Bake on the middle shelf of the preheated oven for about 20 minutes until the pastry is light golden and crisp.

Leave to cool then dust with icing sugar before serving.

MINI PASSION FRUIT & LIME MERINGUE PIES

Delightfully tangy – but at the same time offering sweet curd, crisp,
buttery pastry and light-as-air meringue – these little tarts do not need
to be any larger than their diminutive size. They pack quite a punch – the
sweetest punch possible – but punchy all the same. If you don't have little
tartlet tins, a 12-hole muffin tin will suffice.

Sweet pastry
200g [1½ cups] plain [all-purpose]
　　flour plus extra for rolling out
a pinch of salt
125g [½ cup plus 1 Tbsp] unsalted
　　butter, chilled and diced
40g [4½ Tbsp] icing
　　[confectioners'] sugar, sifted
1 medium egg yolk
2 Tbsp ice-cold water
2 tsp lemon juice

Passion fruit & lime curd
6 passion fruit
finely grated zest and juice
　　of 2 limes
100g [½ cup minus 1 Tbsp]
　　unsalted butter, diced
150g [¾ cup] caster [granulated]
　　sugar
1 medium egg, plus 4 medium
　　yolks (save the whites for the
　　meringue)
a pinch of salt

Italian meringue
2 medium egg whites
a pinch of salt
100g [½ cup] caster [superfine]
　　sugar
50ml [3½ Tbsp] water

You will need a 9–10-cm
　　[3½–4-in] plain round cutter
　　and 12 x 6–7-cm [2½–2¾-in]
　　tartlet tins, 2.5cm [1in] deep;
　　a piping [pastry] bag fitted
　　with a 1-cm [³/₈-in] ribbon
　　nozzle [tip]; a sugar
　　thermometer; a kitchen
　　blowtorch

Makes 12

Prepare the sweet pastry following the instructions on
page 11 and chill for at least 2 hours until firm.

While the pastry is resting, prepare the curd. Cut the
passion fruit in half and scoop the seeds and juice into a
medium-sized heatproof glass or ceramic bowl. Add the
lime zest and juice, butter and sugar. Add the whole egg
and extra yolks and whisk well to combine.

Set the bowl over a pan of gently simmering water,
making sure the bottom of the bowl does not come into
contact with the water (or the heat will scramble the eggs).
Stir the mixture constantly until the butter melts, the
sugar dissolves, the eggs cook and the curd reaches the
consistency of very thick custard.

Remove from the heat, strain into a clean bowl then
sit the bowl in a sink of cold water to speed up the
cooling process, stirring occasionally until cold. Cover
the surface of the curd with cling film [plastic wrap] and
chill until ready to use.

Roll out the dough on a lightly floured surface to
a thickness of about 2mm [¹/₁₆in]. Using the cutter,
stamp out as many rounds as you can from the dough.
Gather any scraps together, press into a ball, roll out
again and stamp out more rounds. You should be able
to get 12 rounds.

Press the pastry rounds into the tartlet tins, making sure
that the pastry neatly fits into the corners. Prick the bases

continued »

SWEET

29

continued »

with a fork and chill for 20 minutes while
you preheat the oven to 170°C/330°F/
Gas 3½. Place a solid baking sheet on the
middle shelf of the oven as it heats.

Line each pastry case with foil and fill
with baking rice. Carefully slide the tins
onto the hot baking sheet and bake for
12 minutes until the pastry edges are
golden. Remove the foil and rice and bake
for a further 2 minutes to crisp the bases.

Spoon the curd into the pastry cases,
filling them almost to the top, and return
to the oven for 2 minutes. Remove from
the oven and leave to cool. Once cold,
remove the tarts from the tins and arrange
on a baking sheet.

To make the meringue, tip the egg whites
into the bowl of a free-standing mixer
fitted with a whisk attachment and add the
salt. Put the sugar into a small saucepan
and add the water. Set the pan over a low
heat to dissolve the sugar, pop the sugar
thermometer into the pan and bring the
syrup to the boil. Continue bubbling until
the syrup reaches 120°C/250°F on the
sugar thermometer. Working quickly, whisk
the egg whites until they just hold a stiff
peak then carefully pour the hot syrup into
the bowl, whisking constantly. Continue
whisking until the meringue mix is cool,
stiff and glossy white.

Scoop the meringue into the piping
bag and pipe swirls on top of each pie.
Scorch the tops with a blowtorch, being
careful not to over-singe or set fire to the
meringue. Leave for 20 minutes or so and
then serve.

PASTEIS DE NATA

You can spot a good Portuguese bakery by the length of queues snaking out of the door – and most likely the queues will be for custard tarts, which have gained something of a cult status in recent years.

OK – I do appreciate that these are possibly not the easiest custard tarts to make, but I don't live in Lisbon or near any good Portuguese bakeries so have to make my own.

They do require a modicum of effort in the pastry-making department, but really this recipe is no harder than making puff pastry. When you pull these tarts out of the oven you will be happy that you took up the challenge.

Pastry
175g [1⅓ cups] plain [all-purpose]
    flour, plus extra for rolling out
100g [¾ cup minus 1 Tbsp] strong
    white flour
a good pinch of sea salt
170ml [⅔ cup plus 2 teaspoons]
    ice-cold water
2 tsp lemon juice
160g [¾ cup minus 2 tsp] unsalted
    butter, softened
½ tsp ground cinnamon

Filling
275g [1½ cups] caster [granulated]
    sugar
150ml [⅔ cup] water
½ vanilla pod [bean], split
    in half lengthways
1 cinnamon stick
3 pared strips of lemon zest
2 pared strips of orange zest
300ml [1¼ cups] whole milk
3 Tbsp cornflour [cornstarch]
a pinch of salt
8 medium egg yolks

You will need 10 x 7-cm [2¾-in]
    straight-sided tart tins or a
    12-hole muffin tin (preferably
    non-stick)

Makes 20

Start by making the pastry – ideally this needs to be prepared the day before you plan on making the tarts, or at least early in the morning before an afternoon of baking to allowing for maximum chilling time.

Combine both flours and the salt in a mixing bowl, add the water and lemon juice and mix, first using a rubber spatula and then your hands until it becomes a smooth dough. Cover the bowl with a clean tea towel and leave to rest for 30 minutes.

Dust the work surface with flour, turn the dough out of the bowl and shape into a neat square. Roll the dough into a neat rectangle three times as long as it is wide – roughly 36 x 12cm [14 x 5in] – and with one of the shorter sides closest to you. Try to keep all the sides as neat as possible when rolling. Using the rolling pin, squash three-quarters of the butter in between 2 sheets of baking parchment, into a square that is slightly smaller than one-third of the dough rectangle, i.e. 10–11cm [4–4½in] square.

Place the butter squarely in the middle third of the dough rectangle and fold the top third down onto the middle, covering the butter, and the bottom third up over to cover that. Press the edges together to seal in the butter.

continued »

SWEET

31

continued »

You will now have a neat square with 3 layers of dough and 1 layer of butter. Turn the square 90° clockwise and, using short, sharp rolling movements, roll the dough out again into a neat rectangle the same size as before. Fold the top third down to the middle again and the bottom third up to cover. Rotate and repeat. Wrap the dough square in baking parchment, slide onto a plate and chill for 1 hour.

Repeat this rolling and folding again so that you will have completed 4 roll and folds. Cover the dough and chill for another hour.

Soften the remaining quarter of butter so that it is very easily spreadable, add the cinnamon and mix to combine. Dust the work surface with flour and roll the dough out into a neat 40-cm [16-in] square. Using a palette knife, spread the cinnamon butter evenly all over the dough. Starting with the side closest to you, roll the dough into a neat, tight spiral log. Cut the log in half to make two short logs, place on a plate, cover and chill for at least 1 hour until very firm.

To make the filling, tip the sugar into a pan, add the water, vanilla pod, cinnamon and lemon and orange zest. Slowly bring to the boil to dissolve the sugar, pop a sugar thermometer into the pan and heat the syrup until it reaches 110°C/225°F.

Whisk a third of the milk with the cornflour and salt in a medium heatproof bowl. Heat the remaining two-thirds of the milk to boiling point then pour the hot milk onto the cold, whisking constantly until smooth.

Slowly add the hot syrup, whisking constantly, then leave to cool for 10 minutes. Beat the egg yolks together in a medium bowl and pour the milk and syrup mixture into the bowl, whisking constantly until smooth. Strain the custard into a clean bowl or jug, leave until cold before covering and chilling until ready to use.

Preheat the oven to 220°C/425°F/Gas 7, positioning the shelf at the top of the oven and placing a solid baking sheet on the shelf to heat up.

I find it easier to make these tarts in batches of 10 at a time. Lightly dust the work surface with flour, trim the end of one of the pastry logs and cut into 1.5-cm [½-in] thick slices. Using the palm and heel of your hand, flatten each slice into a disc with a thickness of about 4mm [1/8in]. With slightly wet or floured fingers, press the pastry discs into the tins, pressing the dough evenly onto the base of the tin and teasing it up the sides. Quickly whisk the custard, as the cornflour may have settled to the bottom of the jug, then pour into the pastry cases, filling each one three-quarters full. Carefully slide the tarts onto the hot baking sheet and cook for 20 minutes until the pastry is golden and crisp and the custard is set and starting to caramelize.

Leave the tarts to cool for a couple of minutes, remove from the tins and transfer to a wire cooling rack. Repeat with the remaining dough and filling.

COCONUT & CHERRY TARTLETS

I like to make these tarts in an assortment of similar sized tart tins, because although I have a vast collection of baking tins I don't stretch to 16 of any one type. These are a little like coconut bakewell tarts minus the overly sweet icing.

Pâte sablée

100g [½ cup minus 1 Tbsp] unsalted butter, at room temperature
50g [5¾ Tbsp] icing [confectioners'] sugar
2 medium egg yolks
1 tsp vanilla extract
175g [1⅓ cups] plain [all-purpose] flour, plus extra for rolling out
a pinch of salt
1 Tbsp double [heavy] cream

Filling

75g [6 Tbsp] soft light brown sugar
75g [6 Tbsp] caster [granulated] sugar
2 medium eggs
3 Tbsp coconut cream
3 Tbsp melted unsalted butter
1 tsp vanilla extract
1 Tbsp plain [all-purpose] flour
125g [1½ cups] unsweetened desiccated [shredded] coconut
a pinch of salt
8 rounded tsp cherry jam
25g [½ cup] unsweetened flaked coconut

You will need 16 deep bun tin moulds or mini brioche tins

Makes 16

To make the pâte sablée, follow the instructions on page 13 and chill for at least 2 hours.

Dust the work surface with flour, divide the pastry into 16 evenly sized balls, roll each ball out to a neat 9-cm [3½-in] round. Line the tart tins with the pastry, trim off any excess and chill for 20 minutes while you preheat the oven to 180°C/350°F/Gas 4.

Meanwhile, to prepare the coconut filling, tip both sugars into a bowl, add the eggs and whisk to combine. Add the coconut cream, melted butter, vanilla, flour, desiccated coconut and salt. Beat well to combine, cover and set aside until ready to bake.

Prick the base of each tart with a fork, place on a baking sheet and bake for 6–7 minutes on the middle shelf of the oven (there is no need to line the tins with foil and rice).

Spoon a rounded ½ teaspoon of the jam into each tart shell, cover with coconut filling and sprinkle the coconut flakes on top. Bake for 16 minutes until risen and golden brown. Leave to cool for a few minutes, then remove the tarts from the tins and cool on a wire rack.

POP TARTS

Fill these little tarts with whatever you like really – I tend to use a variety of fillings as I am seriously indecisive (and greedy), so go for a mixture of either jam, Nutella or a combination of Nutella and toffee sauce.

Pastry
200g [1½ cups] plain [all-purpose] flour, plus extra for rolling out
a pinch of salt
125g [½ cup plus 1 Tbsp] unsalted butter, chilled and diced
3 Tbsp malted milk powder
1 Tbsp icing [confectioners'] sugar, plus extra for dusting
2 Tbsp ice-cold water
1 tsp vanilla extract
1 tsp lemon juice
1 Tbsp milk, for sealing and glazing

Filling
12–14 teaspoons jam, Nutella, or a mixture of Nutella and dulce de leche

To finish
50g [2oz] white chocolate, melted
sprinkles

You will need a 7-cm [2¾-in] plain round cutter and a 7.5-cm [3-in] plain round cutter

Makes 12

To make the pastry, tip the flour into a large mixing bowl and add the salt. Add the diced butter and cut into the flour using a palette or butter knife until all of the butter cubes are at least half their original size and are well coated in flour. Switch to using your hands to rub the butter into the flour until only very small flecks of butter remain and the mixture resembles fine breadcrumbs. Sift the malted milk powder and icing sugar into the bowl and mix again to thoroughly combine.

Sprinkle the water, vanilla and lemon juice over the dry ingredients and mix to combine, first using a palette knife and then switching to your hands. Do not overwork the dough, but bring together into a neat, smooth ball. Flatten into a disc, cover with cling film [plastic wrap] and chill for 1 hour.

Roll the pastry out on a lightly floured surface to a thickness of 2mm [1/16in]. Using both cutters, stamp out an even number of large and small rounds from the pastry. Gather the off-cuts into a ball and re-roll and stamp out more rounds. Lay the smaller rounds on a baking sheet lined with baking parchment.

Now fill your pop tarts with jam, Nutella or a mixture of Nutella and dulce de leche. Spoon 1 rounded teaspoon of your chosen filling into the middle of each smaller round, leaving a border all around of 1cm [⅜in]. Brush the border with milk and top with the larger pastry rounds. Press the edges together to seal, first with your fingers and then using a fork. Chill the pop tarts and preheat the oven to 170°C/330°F/Gas 3½.

Brush the top of the pop pies with milk and bake on the middle shelf of the oven for 20 minutes until golden brown. Leave to cool slightly, then drizzle with melted white chocolate and adorn with sprinkles.

S'MORES TARTLETS

S'mores are a classic campfire treat hailing from North America which have, for good reason, now become a 'thing' across the pond too. I've taken the three elements of s'mores – graham crackers, chocolate and marshmallows and combined them to make indulgent bite-sized tarts. The cracker element is now an oaty biscuit pie crust, the chocolate has an extra dazzle of peanut butter and the marshmallows are homemade with a delicate malted flavour.

This recipe makes enough to serve at your next bonfire party, or to celebrate National S'mores Day on August 10.

Oaty biscuits

100g [½ cup minus 1 Tbsp] unsalted butter, softened

50g [¼ cup] soft light brown sugar

1 medium egg yolk (reserve the white for the marshmallows)

1 tsp vanilla extract

150g [1 cup plus 2 Tbsp] plain [all-purpose] flour, plus extra for rolling out

30g [4 Tbsp] medium oatmeal

¼ tsp ground cinnamon

a pinch of salt

Chocolate filling

75g [2¾oz] dark [bittersweet] chocolate, finely chopped

50g [1¾oz] milk chocolate, finely chopped

125ml [½ cup] double [heavy] cream

2 Tbsp crunchy peanut butter

1 rounded Tbsp soft light brown sugar

a small pinch of sea salt flakes

ingredients continued »

To make the oaty biscuits, cream the butter with the sugar until soft, pale and light. Add the egg yolk and vanilla and beat again to combine. Tip the flour, oatmeal, cinnamon and salt into the bowl and mix to thoroughly combine. Using your hands, gather the dough together into a neat ball and gently knead for 20 seconds until smooth. Dust the work surface with flour and roll out the dough to a 2–3-mm [1/16–1/8-in] thickness and, using the cutter, stamp out as many rounds as you can. Gather the off-cuts and scraps back together into a ball, re-roll and stamp out more rounds – you should be able to get 20. Line the tins with the rounds and chill for 30 minutes while you preheat the oven to 180°C/350°F/Gas 4.

Prick the base of each tart shell and bake in the middle of the oven for about 12 minutes until crisp and golden. Leave to cool then remove from the tins and arrange the oaty biscuit tart shells on a baking sheet.

Next up make the chocolate filling. Tip both chopped chocolates into a small saucepan. Add the cream, peanut butter, sugar and sea salt flakes. Set the pan over a low heat and stir constantly and gently until smooth, and the chocolate has melted. Spoon the chocolate mixture into the tarts, spread level with the back of a teaspoon and leave to cool to room temperature. Chill until firm.

continued »

Malted marshmallow
2 sheets of platinum-grade leaf
  gelatine
1 medium egg white (reserved
  from the oaty biscuits)
a pinch of salt
100g [½ cup] caster [superfine]
  sugar
1 Tbsp barley malt extract (or
  liquid glucose/golden syrup)
75ml [5 Tbsp] water
1 tsp vanilla extract or bean paste

You will need 2 x 12-hole bun
  tins; an 8–9-cm [3¼–3½-
  in] round cutter; a sugar
  thermometer; a piping [pastry]
  bag fitted with a 1-cm [³/₈-in]
  nozzle [tip]; a kitchen blowtorch

Makes 20

To make the malted marshmallow, soak the gelatine leaves
in a bowl of cold water for about 10 minutes until soft.
Place the egg white in the bowl of a free-standing mixer
fitted with a whisk attachment, add the salt but do not
start mixing just yet.

Tip the sugar and malt extract (or liquid glucose/golden
syrup) into a small saucepan and add the water. Place the
pan over a medium heat and stir gently to dissolve the
sugar. Raise the heat, pop the sugar thermometer into the
pan and bring the mixture to the boil. Continue to cook
at a steady boil until the syrup reaches a temperature of
118°C/244°F (if you don't have a thermometer, this is soft-
ball stage).

While the syrup is cooking, start whisking the egg white
until it will hold a soft peak. With the mixer running
on a medium speed, add the hot syrup to the whisked
egg white in a steady stream. Quickly drain the gelatine,
squeeze the water out, then add to the bowl with the
vanilla. Continue whisking for 4–5 minutes until the
mixture is cool, very glossy white and stiff enough to hold
a firm ribbon trail when the whisk is lifted from the bowl.

Working quickly, scoop the marshmallow into the piping
bag and pipe a generous mound on top of each chocolate
tart. Leave at room temperature for 2 hours for the
marshmallow to set firm.

Just before serving, use the blowtorch to very quickly
scorch the marshmallow.

BLUEBERRY, COCONUT & LIME TARTLETS

In these tarts, the sweetness of the blueberries and the zing from the lime are softened by a cakey frangipane filling with a hint of coconut – which in turn is livened by the lime. You could make this as one larger tart if you prefer – I'd recommend using a 20-cm [8-in] tart tin or ring mould.

Pâte sablée

100g [½ cup minus 1 Tbsp] unsalted butter, at room temperature
50g [5¾ Tbsp] icing [confectioners'] sugar
2 medium egg yolks
1 tsp vanilla extract
175g [1⅓ cups] plain [all-purpose] flour, plus extra for rolling out
a pinch of salt
1 Tbsp double [heavy] cream

Blueberry compote

1 lime
200g [1½ cups] blueberries, plus extra to decorate
2 Tbsp caster [granulated] sugar

Frangipane

125g [½ cup plus 1 Tbsp] unsalted butter, softened
125g [⅔ cup] caster [granulated] sugar
2 medium eggs, lightly beaten
40g [¼ cup] pistachios, plus extra to decorate
40g [½ cup] desiccated [shredded] coconut
20g [¼ cup] ground almonds
1 Tbsp plain [all-purpose] flour
a pinch of salt

Lime syrup & to decorate

3 Tbsp lime juice (about 2 limes)
2 Tbsp caster [granulated] sugar
25g [½ cup] toasted coconut flakes

You will need 8 x 8-cm [3¼-in] tart rings

Makes 8

To make the pâte sablée, follow the instructions on page 13 and chill for at least 1 hour. Then, divide the pastry into 8 equal pieces. Roll out on a lightly floured surface into a round about 2mm [¹/₁₆in] thick and carefully line the tart rings, leaving any excess pastry hanging over the top. Chill for 30 minutes until firm.

Meanwhile, make the blueberry compote. Finely grate the zest from the lime, set aside for the frangipane and squeeze the juice. Tip the blueberries, lime juice and sugar into a small pan, set over a low heat to dissolve the sugar and continue to cook, stirring frequently, until the berries have burst, thickened and become jammy. Leave to cool.

For the frangipane, cream the butter and sugar until pale and light, add the eggs and mix again to combine. Tip the pistachios into a food processor and blend until finely chopped. Add to the creamed butter and sugar mixture along with the desiccated coconut, almonds, reserved lime zest, flour and salt. Mix well until thoroughly combined.

Preheat the oven to 170°C/330°F/Gas 3½. Trim the excess pastry from the top of each tart, prick the bases with a fork, line with foil and fill with baking rice. Bake on the middle shelf for 12 minutes until pale golden. Remove the foil and rice and bake for 2 minutes. Leave the pastry shells to cool slightly. Spread the blueberry compote in the cooled shells. Top with the frangipane (you may have some left over), spread level and bake on for 20 minutes until the filling is golden, risen and just firm.

Meanwhile, make the lime syrup. Heat the lime juice and sugar in a small pan until the sugar has dissolved and the syrup reduced by one-third and slightly thickened. Cool for 5 minutes then brush the syrup on top of each warm tart and leave to cool. Decorate with fresh blueberries, toasted coconut flakes and roughly chopped pistachios.

RASPBERRY ZABAGLIONE TARTLETS

Serve these elegant little tarts at an afternoon tea or as a sophisticated dessert, topped with raspberries, as suggested, or whatever ripe berries happen to be in season. Sliced ripe peaches would also be divine.

Pâte sablée
100g [½ cup minus 1 Tbsp] unsalted butter, at room temperature
50g [5¾ Tbsp] icing [confectioners'] sugar
2 medium egg yolks
1 tsp vanilla extract
175g [1⅓ cups] plain [all-purpose] flour, plus extra for rolling out
a pinch of salt
1 Tbsp double [heavy] cream

Zabaglione filling
4 medium egg yolks
50g [¼ cup] caster [granulated] sugar
3 Tbsp Marsala
a pinch of salt
finely grated zest and juice of ½ lemon
175g [¾ cup] mascarpone
350g [¾lb] raspberries
icing [confectioners'] sugar, for dusting
white chocolate curls to decorate (optional)

You will need 8 x 8-cm [3¼-in] tart rings

Makes 8

Prepare the pâte sablée following the instructions on page 13 and chill for at least 1 hour until firm.

Lightly dust the work surface with flour and divide the dough into 8 even pieces. Roll each piece out into a neat round about 2mm [1/16 in] thick, and use to carefully line the tart rings, leaving any excess pastry hanging over the top. Chill for 30 minutes until firm.

Preheat the oven to 170°C/330°F/Gas 3½.

Trim the excess pastry from the top of each tart, prick the bases with a fork, line with foil and fill with baking rice. Bake on the middle shelf of the oven for 12 minutes until pale golden. Carefully remove the foil and rice and bake for a further 2 minutes to dry out the bases, then leave to cool slightly.

To make the zabaglione filling, put the egg yolks, sugar, Marsala and salt in a medium heatproof ceramic or glass bowl and whisk together using a balloon whisk. Set the bowl over a pan of simmering water and whisk constantly for about 5 minutes until the mixture is hot to the touch, very thick, tripled in volume and the consistency of softly whipped cream or mayonnaise. Remove from the heat and plunge the bottom of the bowl into a sink of cold water to speed up the cooling process. Add the lemon zest and juice and whisk until cold.

Fold the mascarpone into the zabaglione mixture to thoroughly combine. Spoon into the baked tart shells and spread level with the back of a teaspoon. Arrange the raspberries on top, dust with icing sugar and top with white chocolate curls.

SPICED RUBY GRAPEFRUIT
CURD TARTLETS

Grapefruit pairs beautifully with warming spices such as star anise, cardamom and black or pink peppercorns and here I've used this combination to make candied peel to adorn these tartlets. This needs to be prepared at least a day in advance to allow the peels to dry, so bear this in mind. You will end up with more peel than you need but this no bad thing – any extras will keep for weeks in an airtight box or jar and can be added to Eccles Cakes (page 21) or dipped in dark chocolate.

Candied grapefruit peel
1 ruby grapefruit
125g [²/₃ cup] caster [granulated] sugar
1 star anise
1 cardamom pod, bruised
4 black peppercorns, coarsely crushed
150ml [²/₃ cup] water

Pâte sablée
100g [½ cup minus 1 Tbsp] unsalted butter, at room temperature
50g [5¾ Tbsp] icing [confectioners'] sugar
2 medium egg yolks (save the whites for the meringues)
1 tsp vanilla extract
175g [1¹/₃ cups] plain [all-purpose] flour, plus extra for rolling out
a pinch of salt
1 Tbsp double [heavy] cream

ingredients continued »

Start by making the candied peel, which should be prepared the day before you plan to serve the tarts. Cut the grapefruit in half, squeeze the juice, cover and set aside for use in the curd later. Cut the grapefruit peel into 4 pieces, pull away any excess pith and tough membranes and slice the peel into strips 5mm [¼in] wide.

Place the sliced peel in a saucepan, cover with cold water and bring to the boil. Simmer for 2 minutes then drain. Repeat this process a further two times with fresh water each time. (This blanching process softens the grapefruit skin and removes any bitterness.)

Tip the sugar, star anise, cardamom pod and peppercorns into a small, heavy-bottomed saucepan, add the water and place over a medium heat to gently dissolve the sugar. Add the peels to the pan and boil slowly and steadily for about 20 minutes, stirring occasionally until they become soft and translucent and almost all of the syrup has been absorbed. Keep a close eye on the pan for the last 5 minutes as the syrup becomes very thick and can easily burn.

Remove the peels from the pan, lay on a sheet of baking parchment in a single layer and leave to dry overnight, at room temperature.

Prepare the pâte sablée following the instructions on page 13 and chill for at least 1 hour until firm.

continued »

continued »

Ruby grapefruit curd
1 ruby grapefruit
2 cardamom pods, bruised
3 medium egg yolks,
    plus 1 medium egg
125g [²/₃ cup] caster [granulated]
    sugar
a pinch of salt
75g [¹/₃ cup] unsalted butter, diced

Swiss meringue & topping
2 medium egg whites (saved from
    the pastry)
125g [²/₃ cup] caster [superfine]
    sugar
a pinch of salt
2 tsp very finely chopped
    pistachios

You will need 10 x 6-cm [2½-in]
    tart tins; an 8-cm [3¼-in] cutter;
    a kitchen blowtorch

Makes 10

Dust the work surface with flour and roll out the pastry to a thickness of 2mm [¹/₁₆in]. Using the cutter, stamp out as many rounds as you can and line the tart tins. Gather the off-cuts into a ball, re-roll, stamp out more rounds and line more tins. Place on a baking sheet and chill for 30 minutes. Preheat the oven to 180°C/350°F/Gas 4.

Prick the base of each tart shell with a fork and bake on the middle shelf for about 12 minutes until crisp and golden. Leave to cool then remove from the tins.

Finely grate the zest from the grapefruit for the curd into a heatproof ceramic or glass bowl. Squeeze the juice and add to the reserved juice from the candied peels – you will need about 250ml [1 cup] in total. Pour the juice into a small pan, add the bruised cardamom pods and bring to the boil over a medium heat. Continue to boil until there is 150ml [²/₃ cup] juice remaining. Strain into the bowl with the grated zest and leave to cool for 5 minutes.

Add the yolks, whole egg, sugar and salt to the juice and whisk to break up the eggs. Set the bowl over a pan of simmering water, being careful that the bottom of the bowl does not come into contact with the water. Stir frequently to dissolve the sugar and cook for about 10 minutes, stirring often, until the curd has thickened enough to coat the back of the spoon and holds a wobbly ribbon trail when the spoon is lifted from the bowl. Remove the bowl from the heat, add the diced butter and whisk to combine. Pass the curd through a fine-mesh sieve into a clean bowl and leave to cool slightly. Then spoon the curd into the tarts, spread level and cool completely.

To make the meringue, whisk the egg whites with the sugar and salt in a medium heatproof bowl. Set the bowl over a pan of simmering water and whisk until the egg whites are glossy, warm to the touch and doubled in volume. Scoop into the bowl of a free-standing mixer and whisk until the meringue will hold a stiff peak. Spoon a swoosh of meringue onto each tart, half covering the curd. Use a blowtorch to scorch the meringue, sprinkle with pistachios, add a strip of candied peel and serve.

SWEET

ETON MESS TARTLETS

I'm not sure that I know a single person who can resist a bowl of
Eton Mess – meringues, cream and strawberries – as it's a winning
combination. I've glammed it up a little here – the cream has become a
silky syllabub that's sweetened with wine and brandy and the meringues
are of course homemade. As you'll have egg whites left over from
making pastry you may as well put them to good use. You'll have more
meringues than you need for 12 little tarts, but I've never found that to be
problematic – just bad for the waistline.

These delicate little tarts are ideal to serve as part of an afternoon tea but
can be made into larger 8-cm [3¼-in] tarts for dessert if you prefer – you
will get 8 tarts rather than 12.

Pâte sablée
100g [½ cup minus 1 Tbsp]
　unsalted butter, at room
　temperature
50g [5¾ Tbsp] icing
　[confectioners'] sugar
2 medium egg yolks (save the
　whites for the meringues)
1 tsp vanilla extract
175g [1⅓ cups] plain [all-purpose]
　flour, plus extra for rolling out
a pinch of salt
1 Tbsp double [heavy] cream

Meringue kisses
2 medium egg whites (saved from
　pastry making, roughly 60g/2oz)
130g [⅔ cup] caster [superfine]
　sugar
2 tsp water
a pinch of salt

ingredients continued »

Prepare the pâte sablée following the instructions on
page 13 and chill for at least 1 hour until firm.

Meanwhile, make the meringue kisses. Preheat the
oven to 110°C/225°F/Gas ¼ and line a baking sheet
with baking parchment.

Tip the egg whites into a medium, heatproof glass or
ceramic bowl and add the sugar, water and salt. Set the
bowl over a pan of simmering water but do not allow
the bottom of the bowl to come into contact with the
hot water.

Using a balloon whisk, beat the egg whites and sugar
until thoroughly combined. Continue whisking over the
simmering water for about 5 minutes until the sugar has
completely dissolved, the mixture has turned from opaque
to white and is hot to the touch.

Quickly pour the mixture into the bowl of a free-standing
mixer and whisk on a medium–high speed for about
3 minutes until the meringue is thick, glossy and white
and will stand in stiff peaks. Scoop the meringue into
the piping bag fitted with the star nozzle and pipe little
meringue kisses in neat rows on the baking parchment.

Bake on the middle shelf of the oven for 40 minutes until
crisp. Turn off the oven, leaving the meringues inside.

continued »

continued »

Syllabub
50ml [3½ Tbsp] Muscat or sweet
    white wine
1 Tbsp brandy
finely grated zest and juice
    of ½ lemon
2 Tbsp caster [superfine] sugar
350ml [1½ cups] double [heavy]
    cream
400g [14oz] small strawberries

You will need 12 tart tins with
    a base measurement of 6cm
    [2½in]; a 9-cm [3½-in] round
    cutter, a piping [pastry] bag
    fitted with a 1-cm [3/8-in] open
    star nozzle [tip]

Makes 12

To make the syllabub base, in a small bowl whisk together the Muscat or sweet wine, brandy, lemon zest and juice and add the sugar. Mix to dissolve the sugar, cover and set aside for an hour or so.

Dust the work surface with flour and roll out the pastry to a thickness of 2–3mm/$^{1}/_{16}$–$^{1}/_{8}$ in. Using the cutter, stamp out as many rounds as you can from the pastry. Gather the scraps together into a ball, re-roll and stamp out more rounds. Carefully line the tart tins with the pastry rounds, arrange on a baking sheet and chill for 30 minutes while you preheat the oven to 180°C/350°F/Gas 4 (having taken the cooled meringues out first).

Prick the base of each tartlet with a fork and bake on the middle shelf for about 12 minutes until crisp and golden. Remove from the oven and leave to cool.

Pick out the smallest, prettiest strawberries and set aside; you will need one for each tart, depending on size. Hull and quarter the remainder, tip into a bowl and add 2 tsp of the syllabub base. Leave to macerate for 30 minutes and then mash the strawberries with a fork into a rough purée.

Pour the cream into a bowl and, whisking slowly and constantly, pour in the syllabub base in a continuous stream. The cream will thicken into soft folds – do not over-whisk. Take out 2 tablespoons of syllabub and set aside. Fold the mashed strawberries into the remaining syllabub and divide between the tart cases. Sandwich 16 meringue kisses with the reserved syllabub and place 2 pairs on top of each tart, along with a quartered strawberry. Dust with icing sugar and serve.

Note: If you prefer to make the syllabub alcohol-free, simply use a glug of elderflower cordial/syrup instead of the wine and brandy.

BITTER ORANGE & BAY CURD TARTS

I've always loved citrus curd tarts – I think it's a throwback to the mini lemon curd tarts my mother made us as a teatime treat when we were very little. These tarts are a major step forward in sophistication from those childhood treats. They are filled with a caramelized orange curd that's delicately scented with bay. Orange and fresh bay leaves are a wonderful combination – the bay adds a subtle herbal note to the lip-smacking orange caramel.

For a decorative flourish, make candied orange peel: simply simmer julienned strips of peel in sugar syrup until they are sticky and start to become translucent. Remove from the syrup and leave to dry out on baking parchment.

Pâte sablée

100g [½ cup minus 1 Tbsp] unsalted butter, at room temperature
50g [5¾ Tbsp] icing [confectioners'] sugar
2 medium egg yolks (save 1 egg white for sealing the pastry)
1 tsp vanilla extract
175g [1⅓ cups] plain [all-purpose] flour, plus extra for rolling out
a pinch of salt
1 Tbsp double [heavy] cream

Curd filling

225g [1¼ cups] caster [granulated] sugar
2 Tbsp hot water
juice of 2 large oranges
1 fresh bay leaf
2 large eggs, plus 4 large yolks
100g [½ cup minus 1 Tbsp] unsalted butter, diced
100g [3½oz] crème fraîche, plus extra to serve
2 tsp lemon juice
a pinch of salt

You will need 6 x 10-cm [4-in] tart tins

Makes 6

Prepare the pâte sablée following the instructions on page 13 and chill for at least 1 hour until firm.

Meanwhile, prepare the filling. Tip 125g [¾ cup] of the sugar into a medium-sized saucepan, add the water and set the pan over a low heat to slowly dissolve the sugar. Once the sugar has completely dissolved increase the heat, bring the syrup to the boil and continue to bubble until it becomes a deep amber coloured caramel. You may need to brush any sugar crystals from the side of the pan with a wet pastry brush as the syrup reduces. Working quickly and carefully, slide the pan off the heat and slowly add the orange juice – the caramel will hiss and bubble violently. Add the bay leaf, return the pan to a medium heat and stir until smooth and the caramel has melted into the juice. Simmer for about 20 minutes until the mixture has reduced to about 200ml [generous ¾ cup]. Remove the bay leaf.

Put the eggs and extra yolks into a medium heatproof bowl and add the remaining 100g [½ cup] sugar.

Whisk to combine then add the diced butter and orange syrup. Set the bowl over a pan of simmering water and cook, stirring often, until the butter has melted, the curd is hot to the touch and thickens enough to coat the back of a spoon. Remove the bowl from the heat, strain the

continued »

continued »

curd into a clean bowl, add the crème fraîche, lemon juice and a pinch of salt and leave to cool.

Cut the chilled pastry into 6 evenly sized pieces. Roll each piece out on a lightly floured surface into a round about 2mm [1/16in] thick and at least 4cm [1½in] wider in diameter than the tart tins. Carefully line the tart tins with the pastry rounds and chill on a baking sheet for 20–30 minutes while you preheat the oven to 180°C/350°F/Gas 4.

Trim the excess pastry from the tarts, line with foil, fill with baking rice and bake on the middle shelf for about 12 minutes until the top edges are golden. Remove the foil and rice and continue to cook for a further 2 minutes to dry out the bases. Lightly beat the reserved egg white, brush onto the base of each tart shell and bake for a further minute to create a seal.

Reduce the oven temperature to 150°C/ 300°F/Gas 2.

Divide the curd between the pastry cases and bake for a further 12–15 minutes until just set. Leave to cool to room temperature.

Once cold, remove the tarts from the tins and serve with some candied orange peel (see introduction) and crème fraîche.

SWEET

MARSALA PEAR
& HAZELNUT TARTS

Serve these elegant tarts with either crème fraîche or a tub of the best
ice cream – vanilla or chocolate, or perhaps a scoop of both.

As I don't like waste in the kitchen, I fiddled around and found a use for
the Marsala poaching syrup. Reduced down to a sticky syrup with just a
hint of bitter chocolate, it can either be served alongside these tarts, or
drizzled over ice cream.

500g [1lb 2oz] all-butter
  puff pastry (see page 12
  for homemade)
plain [all-purpose] flour,
  for rolling out
50g [1¾oz] dark [bittersweet]
  chocolate (70% cocoa solids)
1 medium egg, beaten

Marsala poached pears
4 firm pears, such as Conference
  or Williams
300ml [1¼ cups] Marsala
75g [6 Tbsp] light muscovado
  sugar
pared zest and juice of ½ lemon
½ plump vanilla pod [bean]
about 200ml [generous ¾ cup]
  water

Hazelnut frangipane
75g [scant ½ cup] blanched
  hazelnuts, toasted
50g [3½ Tbsp] unsalted butter,
  at room temperature
50g [¼ cup] caster [granulated]
  sugar
2 tsp plain [all-purpose] flour
2 medium egg yolks
1 tsp vanilla extract
1 tsp finely grated lemon zest
a pinch of salt

You will need a 14-cm [5½-in]
  saucer and an 8-cm [3¼-in]
  plain round cutter

Makes 8

To make the Marsala poached pears, peel the pears, keeping the stalk intact, and place in a medium saucepan in which they will fit snugly. Pour over the Marsala, add the sugar, lemon zest and juice. Split the vanilla pod in half lengthways to expose the seeds and add both halves to the pan, along with enough of the water to just cover the pears.

Set the pan over a low–medium heat and slowly bring to a simmer to dissolve the sugar. Simmer for about 20 minutes until the pears are just tender – think al dente; the cooking time will depend largely on the ripeness and firmness of the pears. Remove the pan from the heat and leave the pears to cool in the syrup. When the pears are cold, remove from the pan using a slotted spoon, and set aside.

Bring the poaching liquid to the boil and cook at a steady bubble until the syrup has reduced to about 8 tablespoons of sticky glaze. Remove the vanilla pod halves and lemon zest.

Prepare the hazelnut frangipane. Whizz the toasted hazelnuts in a food processor until finely chopped. Add the remaining ingredients and blend again until thoroughly combined.

Cut the pears in half and carefully remove the cores using a teaspoon or melon baller, and leave the halves to drain on kitchen paper [paper towels] for a few minutes.

Dust the work surface with plain flour and divide the pastry into 8 evenly sized pieces. Roll each piece out to a neat square with a thickness of 2–3mm [¹/₁₆–¹/₈in]. Using the saucer as a guide, cut out a 14-cm [5½-in] round from each piece of pastry. Knock up the sides of each round

continued »

continued »

(see page 135) using a small, sharp knife, arrange on a baking sheet lined with baking parchment and chill for 20 minutes while you preheat the oven to 180°C/350°F/Gas 4.

Using the 8-cm [3¼-in] plain cutter, press a circle mark into each pastry round, cutting into but not through the pastry. Spoon the frangipane onto each pastry round spreading it to fill the inner circle markers. Chop half of the chocolate into 8 little squares and press one nugget into the middle of the frangipane. Brush the exposed pastry border with beaten egg and arrange a pear half on top.

Bake for 30 minutes then remove from the oven, brush with the reserved, reduced syrup and return to the oven for a further 5–6 minutes until caramelized.

Warm the remaining syrup over a low heat, add the remaining chocolate and gently heat to melt, but do not allow to boil or the chocolate will burn. Stir until smooth and keep warm.

Leave the tarts to cool down to room temperature and serve with the warm chocolate syrup drizzled over the top, and perhaps with a scoop of ice cream.

CHOCOLATE & HAZELNUT
SALTED CARAMEL TARTS

What did we do before salted caramel? A dense, rich chocolate fudgey filling sits atop a hazelnut-studded caramel before being adorned with caramel-coated hazelnuts. The extra spiky caramel hazelnuts do take a little practice and don't like to be in a humid atmosphere, which can soften the caramel, so make them as close to serving as you dare.

Pastry
125g [½ cup plus 1 Tbsp] unsalted butter, softened
75g [½ cup] icing [confectioners'] sugar, sifted
a pinch of salt
1 tsp vanilla extract
1 medium egg, lightly beaten
225g [1¾ cups] plain [all-purpose] flour, plus extra for rolling out
40g [1½oz] cocoa powder

Caramel
75g [6 Tbsp] caster [granulated] sugar
1 Tbsp hot water
25g [1¾ Tbsp] unsalted butter
100ml [⅓ cup plus 1 Tbsp] double [heavy] cream
1 Tbsp golden syrup
a large pinch of sea salt flakes
75g [½ cup] blanched hazelnuts, toasted

ingredients continued »

Start by making the pastry. Cream the butter, sugar and salt together in a free-standing mixer using the paddle or K-shaped attachment for a couple of minutes until pale. Add the vanilla extract and mix again. Gradually add the beaten egg, mixing well between each addition until fully incorporated. Sift the flour and cocoa into the bowl and gently mix in using a rubber spatula but do not overwork the mixture. Bring the dough together into a ball, flatten into a disc, wrap in cling film [plastic wrap] and chill for 1 hour until firm. Then, divide the pastry into 8 even pieces and roll each piece out on a lightly floured work surface, line the tart tins and trim off the excess from the top of each. Chill the pastry shells for 30 minutes while you preheat the oven to 180°C/350°F/Gas 4.

Prick the base of each tart shell with a fork, line with foil and fill with baking rice. Bake the tart shells on the middle shelf of the oven for about 12 minutes until crisp. Remove the foil and rice and cook for a further minute to dry out the base of each tart shell. Reduce the oven temperature to 170°C/330°F/Gas 3½.

Next prepare the caramel. Tip the sugar into a small pan, add the hot water and heat gently to dissolve the sugar. Increase the heat and cook until the sugar turns to a rich amber caramel. Slide the pan off the heat, carefully add the butter, cream and golden syrup, return the pan to a low heat and stir until smooth and thickened. Simmer for 1 minute, remove from the heat and add the salt.

Leave to cool for 2 minutes and spread the caramel into the tart shells. Chop the hazelnuts, sprinkle over the caramel and set aside.

continued »

continued »

Filling
100g [3½oz] dark [bittersweet] chocolate (70% cocoa solids), chopped
75g [⅓ cup] unsalted butter
2 medium eggs plus 1 medium yolk
50g [¼ cup] caster [granulated] sugar
1 Tbsp cocoa powder, sifted

Glaze
50g [1¾oz] dark [bittersweet] chocolate, chopped
25g [1¾ Tbsp] unsalted butter
2 Tbsp whole milk
1 tsp golden syrup

Hazelnut spikes
50g [⅓ cup] blanched hazelnuts
150g [¾ cup] caster [granulated] sugar
1 Tbsp hot water

To finish
25g [1oz] dark [bittersweet] chocolate

You will need 8 x 10-cm [4-in] tartlet tins

Makes 8

For the filling, melt the chocolate and butter in a heatproof bowl over a pan of simmering water, stir until smooth, remove from the heat and cool slightly. In a separate bowl, whisk the eggs, egg yolk and sugar until thick and pale. Using a large metal spoon or rubber spatula, fold in the melted chocolate with the cocoa until well combined – the mixture will lose a lot of volume. Divide the filling between the tart cases, bake for 7–8 minutes until just set, then cool to room temperature.

For the glaze, mix the ingredients in a small pan and warm over a moderate heat, stirring until smooth and shiny. Remove from the heat, cool for 1 minute and spoon over each tart to cover evenly. Allow to set.

For the hazelnut spikes, carefully press a cocktail stick [toothpick] into each hazelnut and set aside. Cover the work surface with baking parchment. Tip the sugar into a small, solid-bottomed pan and add the water. Set over a low heat to dissolve the sugar, without stirring. Bring the syrup to a boil and cook until it becomes an amber caramel. Remove from the heat and cool slightly. One at a time, dip each hazelnut into the caramel to coat and then hold over the pan to allow the excess to drip into a long, elegant tail. If you have a shelf above your work surface it'll be very useful at this moment. Wedge each skewer under something so that the caramel tail is hanging over the edge and dripping onto the parchment. Alternatively, lay them flat on the parchment to set. When set, gently remove the sticks. If the caramel in the pan starts to harden simply place it back over a gentle heat to soften again.

To finish, melt the chocolate, spoon into a disposable piping bag and snip the end into a fine point. Pipe delicate lines across each tart and, just before serving, decorate with 3 spiky caramel hazelnuts.

CRÈME BRÛLÉE TARTS WITH ANISE-ROASTED BLACKBERRIES

I love crème brûlée – who doesn't? The combination of silky custard, bitter caramel and the drama of smashing through the glassy caramel with your spoon is irresistible. I like to serve super creamy puds with something fruity to cut through the decadence, and anise-roasted blackberries fit the bill nicely.

This method for making crème brûlée makes for an unctuous filling, but it does require some patience – don't be tempted to rush this stage otherwise the eggs will not cook and the custard won't set.

Pâte sablée

100g [½ cup minus 1 Tbsp] unsalted butter, at room temperature
50g [5¾ Tbsp] icing [confectioners'] sugar
2 medium egg yolks
1 tsp finely grated lemon zest
175g [1⅓ cups] plain [all-purpose] flour, plus extra for rolling out
a pinch of salt
1 Tbsp double [heavy] cream

Crème brûlée

500ml [generous 2 cups] double [heavy] cream
1 vanilla pod [bean], split in half lengthways
5 medium egg yolks
50g [¼ cup] caster [granulated] sugar, plus 8 tsp for caramelizing
25g [1¾ Tbsp] unsalted butter, diced

Roasted blackberries

300g [10½oz] blackberries
2–3 tsp caster [granulated] sugar
juice of ½ lemon
½ tsp anise seeds or 2 star anise

You will need 8 x 8-cm [3¼-in] tart rings and a kitchen blowtorch

Makes 8

Prepare the pâte sablée following the instructions on page 13 and adding the lemon zest in with the flour. Chill for at least 2 hours.

Dust the work surface with flour, divide the dough into 8 equal portions, roll each out into a neat round and line the tart rings. Chill for 30 minutes while you preheat the oven to 180°C/350°F/Gas 4.

Prick the base of the tart shells with a fork, line with foil, fill with baking rice and bake on the middle shelf of the oven for about 14 minutes until pale golden. Remove the foil and rice and continue to cook for a further 2 minutes to dry out and crisp the bases. Leave to cool.

Pour the cream for the crème brûlée into a saucepan and add the halved vanilla pod. Bring slowly to the boil then remove from the heat and leave to infuse for 30 minutes.

Whisk together the egg yolks, sugar and a pinch of salt in a medium heatproof bowl. Set the bowl over a pan of simmering water; do not allow the bottom of the bowl to come into contact with the water or the eggs will scramble. Whisk constantly until the sugar has dissolved. Bring the cream back to the boil, pour onto the egg yolk mixture, whisking constantly until smooth. Continue to cook the custard in the bain-marie for about 10 minutes, stirring with a rubber spatula until the custard is hot and

continued »

continued »

thickened enough to coat the back of a spoon. It might feel as it will never thicken, but suddenly the bubbles on top of the custard disappear, the vanilla seeds are suspended and the mixture turns into silky, thick custard.

Remove from the heat, add the diced butter and stir gently to combine. Strain the custard into a jug and pour into the tart shells, filling them all the way to the top. Leave to cool to room temperature. Arrange the tarts in a deep tray and cover the tray with cling film [plastic wrap], making sure it isn't touching the top of the custard. Chill for at least 8 hours or overnight until ready to serve.

Preheat the oven to 180°C/350°F/Gas 4. Tip the blackberries into a roasting tray, add the sugar, lemon juice and anise and stir to combine. Cover loosely with foil and bake on the middle shelf for about 10 minutes until the berries are tender and juicy. Leave to cool to room temperature.

Spread 1 teaspoon of sugar evenly over the top of each of the custard-filled tarts. Use a blowtorch to caramelize the sugar, being careful not to scorch the pastry edges. Return the tarts to the fridge for 30 minutes to allow the crème brûlée filling to firm up.

Serve each tart with a spoonful of roasted blackberries.

RHUBARB & STRAWBERRY GALETTES

You might think this a curious combination, but rhubarb and strawberries baked in a pie is something I first came across many moons ago while working in the USA – that pie was called Rhuberry Pie. And the pairing really works – the sweetness of the strawberries contrasting with the tartness of the rhubarb. Look out for forced, tender stemmed, neon pink rhubarb – not only because it looks pretty but because it'll cook faster and be slightly sweeter than its outdoor-grown cousin.

Serve these galettes with a generous dollop of lightly whipped cream or vanilla ice cream.

Cream cheese pastry
150g [1 cup plus 2 Tbsp] plain [all-purpose] flour, plus extra for rolling out
½ tsp baking powder
2 Tbsp caster [granulated] sugar
a pinch of salt
75g [⅓ cup] unsalted butter, chilled and diced
75g [⅓ cup] cream cheese, chilled
50g [½ cup] ground almonds
1 medium egg yolk (save the white for glazing)
1 Tbsp cold milk or water

Filling
350g [¾lb] forced rhubarb, trimmed
350g [¾lb] ripe strawberries, trimmed
juice of ½ lemon
1 tsp vanilla bean paste
3 Tbsp caster [granulated] sugar, plus extra for sprinkling
1 Tbsp ground almonds

Makes 6

Prepare the cream cheese pastry following the instructions on page 13 and chill for at least 1 hour.

Cut the rhubarb diagonally into 3-cm [1¼-in] lengths and the strawberries in half or quarters, depending on size. Tip the fruit into a bowl with the lemon juice, vanilla and sugar, mix to combine and set aside for 20 minutes to allow the sugar to dissolve and the fruit to become juicy.

Preheat the oven to 180°C/350°F/Gas 4.

Lightly dust the work surface with flour and divide the dough into 6 even pieces. Shape each piece into a disc and roll out into a neat 15–17-cm [6–7-in] round. Lay the pastry rounds on the work surface and sprinkle the ground almonds over the middle of each. Mound the rhubarb and strawberries in the middle of each pastry, leaving a 3-cm [1¼-in] border all around. Fold the pastry up and around the fruit to form a ridge with the filling exposed, and drizzle over any juice left in the bowl. Transfer the tarts to a baking sheet lined with baking parchment.

Brush the pastry edges with lightly beaten egg white, sprinkle generously with sugar and bake on the middle shelf of the oven for 25 minutes. Lower the temperature to 170°C/330°F/Gas 3½ and cook for a further 5–10 minutes until the pastry is golden and crisp and the fruit is tender, juicy and bubbling.

FLORENTINE-TOPPED TARTS

Florentines are more often seen at Christmas time with their jewel-like dried fruit and nuts all held together by a chewy caramel and bottoms dunked in dark chocolate. These tarts wouldn't look out of place on a festive table either. Buttery pastry filled with a spiced, light frangipane and topped with candied fruit and nuts. They are generously proportioned but no one who's tried them has found this to be much of a hurdle. This might be one of my favourite recipes in the book.

Sweet pastry

200g [1½ cups] plain [all-purpose] flour

a pinch of salt

125g [½ cup plus 1 Tbsp] unsalted butter, chilled and diced

40g [4½ Tbsp] icing [confectioners'] sugar

1 medium egg yolk (save the white for sealing the pastry)

2 Tbsp ice-cold water

2 tsp lemon juice

Filling

1 medium egg, plus 1 medium egg yolk

75g [6 Tbsp] caster [granulated] sugar

75g [¾ cup] ground almonds

25g [3 Tbsp] plain [all-purpose] flour

¼ tsp ground cardamom

1 tsp finely grated orange zest

a good pinch of salt

25g [1¾ Tbsp] unsalted butter, melted

Florentine topping

50g [1¾oz] glacé cherries

50g [1¾oz] candied mixed peel

75g [scant 1 cup] flaked [slivered] almonds

40g [1½oz] slivered pistachios

75g [⅓ cup] unsalted butter

75g [6 Tbsp] soft light brown or demerara sugar

2 Tbsp double [heavy] cream

1 Tbsp clear honey

a pinch of salt

You will need 6 x 10-cm [4-in] deep fluted tart tins with removable bases

Makes 6

Prepare the sweet pastry following the instructions on page 11 and chill for at least 1 hour.

Dust the work surface with flour, divide the pastry into 6 even portions and roll each out into a round with a thickness of 2–3mm [¹/₁₆–¹/₈in]. Line the tart tins with the pastry, pressing the dough neatly and evenly into the corners and edges. Trim the excess from the top, prick the bases with a fork and chill on a baking sheet while you preheat the oven to 180°C/350°F/Gas 4.

Line the pastry cases with foil, fill with baking rice and cook on the middle shelf of the oven for 18–20 minutes until the top edges are golden. Remove the foil and rice, brush the base of each pie shell with lightly beaten egg white and bake for 1 more minute to seal the pastry.

For the filling, combine the whole egg, extra yolk and sugar in a bowl and whisk until the mixture is pale and doubled in volume. Add the ground almonds, flour, cardamom, orange zest and salt, and fold in. Add the melted butter and stir to mix. Divide the filling between the tart shells, spread level with the back of a spoon and bake for 10–12 minutes until risen and pale golden.

Rinse the glacé cherries to remove any sticky syrup and pat dry on kitchen paper [paper towels]. Quarter and tip into a bowl with the mixed peel, flaked almonds and slivered pistachios. Mix to combine and set aside.

Melt the butter, brown sugar, cream, honey and salt in a small saucepan over a low heat, stirring constantly to prevent the sugar catching on the bottom of the pan. Bring to the boil, simmer for 1 minute, add to the dried fruit and nut mixture and mix to combine.

Spoon the Florentine mixture on top of each tart and return to the oven for a further 12–14 minutes until the nuts are golden and caramelized. Leave to cool for 2 minutes then remove from the tins – if you leave them until cold, any hardened caramel might make it tricky to extricate the tarts from the tins.

SWEET

APPLE & MARZIPAN CHAUSSONS

I love the pairing of apples and buttery pastry – I could have included another five recipes on this theme in this book… These chaussons – or turnovers – are small enough to eat two in one sitting without appearing excessively greedy (unless you are my brother in which case you'd probably eat them all, apples and pastry being almost irresistible to him).

Inside the flaky, buttery pastry layers are softened apple slices and little nuggets of marzipan, and a pinch of cardamom sugar topping is just gilding the lily. A good spoonful of mincemeat stirred into the apples after cooking wouldn't go amiss in these turnovers at Christmas.

After I'd tested this recipe (perhaps more times than necessary) I had the notion to fill the turnovers with nectarines or peaches and blackberries or blackcurrants – but I will wait until they are plentiful and in season.

Puff pastry
250g [1 cup plus 2 Tbsp] unsalted butter, chilled
150g [1 cup plus 2 Tbsp] plain [all-purpose] flour, plus extra for rolling out
100g [¾ cup minus ½ Tbsp] strong white flour
a pinch of salt
1 medium egg yolk
100–125ml [6–8 Tbsp] ice-cold water
1 tsp lemon juice

Filling
5 crisp eating apples, such as Braeburn
2 Tbsp golden caster [granulated] sugar
juice of ½ lemon
1 Tbsp unsalted butter
½ tsp ground cinnamon
½ tsp vanilla bean paste
75g [2¾oz] marzipan, diced
1 egg, beaten
½ tsp ground cardamom
2 Tbsp demerara [turbinado] sugar

You will need a 12-cm [5-in] round cutter or saucer

Makes 14

Prepare the puff pastry either first thing in the morning of the day you plan on baking these apple pies, or better still the day before, following the instructions on page 12. Chill the pastry for at least 1 hour after the final fold.

Peel, quarter and core the apples and cut each quarter into thin slices. Tip the apples into a medium-sized saucepan, add the caster sugar, lemon juice, butter, cinnamon and vanilla. Set the pan over a low–medium heat, stir well to combine, half cover the pan with a lid and cook for 10–15 minutes until the apple slices are really soft and any excess juice has been cooked off. Remove the lid and cook for a few minutes more if the apples are really juicy – you want them to be soft but not watery. Leave to cool.

Dust the work surface with flour and roll out the pastry to a thickness of about 2mm [¹/₁₆in]. Using the cutter or saucer as a guide, stamp out as many rounds as you can from the pastry. Any larger off-cuts can be stacked together and re-rolled to stamp out more rounds; you should get 14 in total.

Lay the pastry rounds on the work surface and spoon a dessertspoonful of the apples on one side of each round, leaving a 1-cm [³/₈-in] border. Scatter diced marzipan over the apples. Lightly brush the border around the apples

continued »

with beaten egg, fold the pastry over to
encase the apples in a half-moon shape
and press the edges together to seal.

Arrange the pastries on a parchment-lined
baking sheet and chill for 15 minutes.
Combine the ground cardamom and
demerara sugar in a small bowl.

Using a paring knife, knock up the
rounded edges of each pastry (see page
135) and brush with beaten egg. Chill the
pastries again for another 15 minutes
while you preheat the oven to 190°C/
375°F/Gas 5.

Brush with egg again and, using the point
of a small, sharp knife, score a decorative
pattern into the top of each pastry –
cutting into but not through the pastry.
Sprinkle over the cardamom sugar and
bake on the middle shelf of the oven for
about 25 minutes, until the pastry is crisp
and a wonderful golden brown.

Serve hot, warm or at room temperature,
with either ice cream or crème fraîche.

SWEET

TIRAMISU DOMES

Now I do appreciate that this recipe has many stages and might look daunting – but the results speak for themselves and almost all the stages can and should be prepared in advance. These are pat-yourself-on-the-back tarts, dance-around-the-kitchen-with-a-grin-on-your-face tarts, and impress-the-in-laws-tarts. And you don't get to be that smug without a little effort.

Buttery pastry is filled with a mascarpone mousse that has just a hint of white chocolate. This is then topped with a dome of milk chocolate and coffee mousse, and a sneaky layer of coffee ganache and crumbled amaretti biscuits. The final layer of chocolate mirror glaze is adorned with a tickle of edible gold leaf. It's not that hard really and you'll be glad you took up the challenge.

However, there are a few rules that simply must not be broken. Prepare the mousses the day before and freeze them in the moulds overnight. While you're at it the glaze, ganache and pastry should be prepared the day before too. The mousses should be glazed very quickly, two at a time, and not allowed to be out of the moulds for longer than about 1 minute before glazing – the glaze will not adhere to the mousse if it has the slightest moisture or condensation on it. Once glazed, leave the mousses in the fridge, uncovered, to defrost for 2 hours and until ready to serve.

Coffee mousse
1 sheet of platinum-strength leaf gelatine
150g [5¼oz] milk chocolate, chopped
25g [1oz] dark [bittersweet] chocolate, at least 64% cocoa solids, chopped
100ml [⅓ cup plus 1 Tbsp] hot espresso or strong coffee
1 Tbsp light muscovado sugar
175ml [¾ cup] double [heavy] cream

Ganache
100ml [⅓ cup plus 1 Tbsp] double [heavy] cream
1 Tbsp Tia Maria or Kahlúa
2 tsp light muscovado sugar
a pinch of salt
125g [4½oz] dark [bittersweet] chocolate, at least 64% cocoa solids, finely chopped
8 crisp amaretti biscuits, finely crushed

Mirror glaze
3 sheets of platinum-strength leaf gelatine
150g [¾ cup] caster [superfine] sugar
50g [½ cup] cocoa powder
100ml [⅓ cup plus 1 Tbsp] double [heavy] cream
1 Tbsp glucose syrup
50ml [3½ Tbsp] water

Pâte sablée
100g [½ cup minus 1 Tbsp] unsalted butter, at room temperature
50g [5¾ Tbsp] icing [confectioners'] sugar
2 medium egg yolks
1 tsp vanilla extract
175g [1⅓ cups] plain [all-purpose] flour, plus extra for rolling out
a pinch of salt
1 Tbsp double [heavy] cream

Mascarpone filling
2 medium egg yolks
25g [2 Tbsp] caster [granulated] sugar
2 Tbsp Tia Maria or Kahlúa
a pinch of salt
250g [generous 1 cup] mascarpone
50g [1¾oz] white chocolate, chopped

To decorate
1 sheet of edible gold leaf

You will need 6 x 8-cm [3¼-in] tart rings, and 6 x 6.5-cm [2½-in] silicone half-sphere moulds

Makes 6

Start with the mousses. Soak the gelatine leaf in a bowl of cold water for 5 minutes until soft. Melt the milk and dark chocolates together in a heatproof bowl over a pan of barely simmering water. Stir until smooth, remove from the heat and leave to cool slightly. Drain the gelatine, squeeze out any excess water and add to the hot coffee with the sugar. Stir to melt the gelatine and dissolve the sugar and leave to cool to room temperature.

Whip the cream to soft, floppy peaks, add the cooled coffee and mix to combine. Fold the melted chocolate into the cream and spoon the mousse into the silicone moulds, spread level, place on a baking sheet and freeze for 2–3 hours until almost firm.

Meanwhile, prepare the ganache. Pour the cream, Tia Maria or Kahlúa, sugar and salt into a small saucepan and bring to the boil over a low heat, stirring to dissolve the sugar.

Tip the chopped chocolate into a bowl, add the hot cream, leave to rest for 1 minute then stir gently in one direction until the ganache is smooth. Leave to firm and cool to room temperature.

Using a melon baller, remove a ball of mousse from the middle of each frozen coffee dome. Fill the space that you've created with ganache and spread more in an even, smooth layer over the flat base of each dome. Sprinkle half of the crushed amaretti in an even layer over the ganache, cover and return the mousses to the freezer overnight, reserving the remaining amaretti in an airtight container.

Next up is the glaze. Soak the gelatine leaves in a bowl of cold water for 5 minutes until soft and floppy. Tip the sugar into a small pan, add the cocoa, cream, glucose syrup and water. Whisking constantly until smooth, bring the mixture to the boil to dissolve the sugar then remove from the heat. Drain the gelatine, shaking off any excess water, and add to the pan. Whisk until the gelatine has melted and thoroughly combined. Pour the glaze into a clean bowl and leave to cool before covering and chilling overnight until needed.

Prepare the pâte sablée following the instructions on page 13 and chill for at least 1 hour until firm.

Dust the work surface with flour, divide the pastry into 6 evenly sized pieces and roll each out into a neat round 2–3mm [$^1/_{16}$–$^1/_8$in] thick. Line the tart rings with pastry, trim any excess from the top, prick the bases with a fork and chill for 30 minutes while you preheat the oven to 180°C/350°F/Gas 4.

Line each pastry shell with foil, fill with baking rice and bake on the middle shelf of the oven for about 12 minutes until golden at the edges. Remove the foil and rice and cook for a further 2 minutes until the pastry is golden brown and the base is crisp. Leave to cool.

Place the glaze over a bowl of hot water to melt for about 1 minute, stirring until smooth. Do not allow it to warm up; it should be smooth and runny but without any heat, so test the temperature with your clean fingertip and leave it too cool slightly if it has heated up. Working quickly, pop two of the mousses out of the moulds and place rounded side uppermost on a cooling rack set over a tray. Carefully spoon the glaze over the top of each mousse so that it runs evenly over the dome. Leave the glaze to set for 1 minute then, using a palette knife, transfer the mousses to a parchment-lined baking sheet and place in the fridge. Repeat with the remaining mousses. Leave the mousses to defrost in the fridge for 2 hours.

To make the mascarpone filling, whisk the egg yolks, sugar, Tia Maria and salt in a medium heatproof ceramic or glass bowl. Set the bowl over a pan of simmering water, without allowing the bottom of the bowl to touch the water, and whisk for about 5 minutes until the mixture is very thick and tripled in volume; it should be the consistency of softly whipped cream or mayonnaise. Remove from the heat and plunge the bottom of the bowl into a sink of cold water to cool.

Melt the white chocolate in a heatproof bowl over the simmering water, stir until smooth then cool slightly. Add the mascarpone to the egg yolk mixture, mix until smooth and fold in the melted white chocolate. Spoon the mascarpone into the baked tart shells and spread level with a palette knife. Chill for 1 hour to firm up slightly.

Carefully lift a glazed mousse on top of each tart, sprinkle the reserved crushed amaretti around the edges and, finally, decorate with a flutter of edible gold leaf.

LEMON & GINGER
POSSET TARTLETS

Lemon posset is possibly the simplest dessert to make, requiring only 3 ingredients. I turn to it time and time again when in need of something quick and elegant that can easily be glammed up with the addition of some delicate berries. I usually serve it with some ginger biscuits – here I've swapped the biscuits for a gingery tart crust and granola topping.

Ginger pastry
125g [½ cup plus 1 Tbsp] unsalted butter, softened
50g [¼ cup] light muscovado sugar
1 Tbsp golden syrup
1 medium egg yolk
150g [1 cup plus 2 Tbsp] plain [all-purpose] flour, plus extra
25g [¼ cup] ground almonds
1 tsp ground ginger
½ tsp ground cinnamon
a grating of nutmeg
a pinch of salt

Granola
50g [⅔ cup] flaked [slivered] almonds
30g [⅓ cup] porridge oats
1 tsp finely grated lemon zest
a pinch of salt
½ tsp ground ginger
¼ tsp ground cinnamon
1 nugget of stem ginger in syrup, drained and finely chopped
1 Tbsp golden syrup
1 Tbsp light muscovado sugar
25g [1¾ Tbsp] unsalted butter

Posset
finely grated zest and juice of 2 lemons
100g [½ cup] caster [granulated] sugar
2 Tbsp syrup from the stem ginger jar
400ml [1⅔ cups] double [heavy] cream

You will need 8 x 8-cm [3¼-in] tart rings

Makes 8

To make the ginger pastry, cream the softened butter, sugar and golden syrup until pale. Add the egg yolk and beat again until thoroughly incorporated. Sift the dry ingredients into the bowl and mix until the dough comes together into a ball, adding a teaspoon or two of ice-cold water if needed. Flatten into a disc, wrap in cling film [plastic wrap] and chill for at least 2 hours.

Dust the work surface with flour, divide the pastry into 8 evenly sized portions and roll each out into a round about 3mm [1/8in] thick. Line the tart rings with the pastry (the pastry is crumblier than normal so patch up any cracks). Trim any excess pastry from the tops of the rings and chill on a baking sheet lined with parchment for 30 minutes.

Preheat the oven to 170°C/330°F/Gas 3½. Prick the tart bases with a fork, line with foil, fill with baking rice and blind bake for 12–14 minutes until the top edges of the tarts are golden. Remove the foil and rice and bake for a further 2 minutes to crisp up the tart bases.

Prepare the granola. Combine the almonds, oats, lemon zest, salt, dry spices and stem ginger in a bowl and mix. Put the golden syrup, sugar and butter into a small pan and melt over a low heat. Swirl the pan, add to the oat mixture and mix. Tip onto a baking sheet lined with baking parchment and bake for 10 minutes until lightly caramelized and golden, stirring twice. Leave to cool.

To make the posset, combine the lemon zest, juice, sugar and ginger syrup in a small saucepan to dissolve the sugar, bring to the boil and remove from the heat. Bring the cream to the boil in another pan, slide off the heat and add the lemon syrup, stirring with a rubber spatula. Pour into the tart shells, leave to cool, then chill for at least 4 hours until set. Serve the tarts topped with the granola.

APPLE ROSE TARTS

These beautiful tarts are filled with a secret ingredient: caramel apple purée. This is essentially just like the roasted caramel apples from my Tarte Tatin recipe on page 77. The apples are cooked until they have slumped into a coma of thick, apple deliciousness and then the purée has many, many uses – you can eat it straight from the pan, dolloped onto yogurt or porridge, slathered into cakes, as a filling for doughnuts, in pies, on pies, with pies… You can thank me later.

The recipe makes more purée than you'll need for these little tarts, but as it's so easy to make it seems pointless making less. It will freeze perfectly for another time.

Caramel apple purée
100g [½ cup] caster [granulated] sugar
25g [1¾ Tbsp] unsalted butter
a pinch of sea salt flakes
6 Golden Delicious apples, peeled, cored and halved

Sweet pastry
200g [1½ cups] plain [all-purpose] flour
a pinch of salt
125g [½ cup plus 1 Tbsp] unsalted butter, chilled and diced
40g [4½ Tbsp] icing [confectioners'] sugar, plus extra for dusting
1 medium egg yolk
2 Tbsp ice-cold water
2 tsp lemon juice

ingredients continued »

Start by preparing the caramel apple purée, which can be cooked well in advance of baking the tarts. Preheat the oven to 190°C/375°F/Gas 5.

Tip the sugar into the skillet or ovenproof frying pan in an even layer and set the pan over a low heat to slowly melt the sugar, without stirring. Continue to cook the sugar until it starts to turn a rich amber-coloured caramel, gently swirling the skillet to ensure that it caramelizes evenly. Add the butter and sea salt flakes and gently stir to melt the butter and combine. Remove from the heat.

Pack the halved apples in a single layer on top of the caramel, cover the skillet tightly with foil and bake on the middle shelf of the oven for 40 minutes. Carefully remove the foil, turn the apples over in the caramel, cover loosely with foil and cook for a further 10 minutes until the apples are super-soft and drenched in appley caramel juices. Set the skillet over a medium–high heat, bubble to cook off any excess syrup and use the back of a spoon to squash and mash the apples into a purée as you do so. Scoop into a bowl, leave to cool then cover and chill until ready to use.

Prepare the sweet pastry following the instructions on page 11 and chill for at least 2 hours.

continued »

SWEET

73

continued »

Nut filling
50g [generous ⅓ cup] blanched
    hazelnuts
50g [generous ⅓ cup] blanched
    almonds
100g [scant ½ cup] unsalted
    butter, at room temperature
100g [½ cup] caster [granulated]
    sugar, plus extra for sprinkling
2 medium eggs
1 Tbsp plain [all-purpose] flour
1 tsp finely grated lemon zest
4 red-skinned apples

You will need a medium-
    sized heavy-based skillet or
    ovenproof frying pan, and
    8 x 8-cm [3¼-in] tartlet rings
    or tins

Makes 8

Divide the dough into 8 equal portions and roll each
piece out on a floured work surface to a thickness of about
2mm [¹/₁₆in], then use to line the tart tins or rings. Trim off
any excess pastry, place on a baking sheet and chill for 30
minutes while you preheat the oven to 180°C/350°F/Gas 4.

Prick the base of each tart, line with foil, fill with baking
rice and blind bake for about 14 minutes until pale golden
at the edges. Remove the foil and bake for a further
minute or two to dry out the bases.

While the pastry is cooking, prepare the nut filling.
Tip the nuts into a food processor and blend until very
finely chopped. Add the softened butter, sugar, eggs,
flour, lemon zest and pinch of salt and blend again until
thoroughly combined.

Spoon 2 teaspoons of caramel apple purée into each tart
shell and spread level. Cover with the nut mixture to fill
each tart three-quarters full. Slice the red apples in half
vertically and remove the core, using a melon baller or
pointed vegetable peeler. Slice each apple half as thinly
as possible into wafer-thin slices. Arrange the apple slices,
skin side uppermost in concentric circles in each tart
shell starting at the outside edge and overlapping them
(like rose petals). Push the slices vertically into the filling
to stand upright, sprinkle with sugar and place back
the baking sheet in the oven to bake for 30 minutes,
until the filling is puffed and golden and the apples
are lightly browned.

Leave to cool to room temperature and dust with icing
sugar to serve.

TARTE TATIN

I wasn't sure that it was necessary to include tarte Tatin in this book – until I ate the TT served at Buvette in New York. The apples were cooked to a melting, caramel-appley tenderness that they were almost translucent and I will admit that I became a little obsessed with how they'd achieved that level of deliciousness. Well, this is how – this slow but simple method of cooking the apples is adapted from that used at Buvette but the cream cheese puff pastry is all mine. This is a classic example of how a few ingredients used well and with care and attention can produce something so utterly sublime. Tarte Tatin is so much more than upside-down caramelized apple tart.

Every time that I write a recipe for any type of puff pastry I cross my fingers and hope that you, dear reader, will actually make it and not take the easy option and open a packet of storebought. Don't let me down!

Pastry
150g [1 cup plus 2 Tbsp] plain [all-purpose] flour, plus extra for rolling out
125g [½ cup plus 1 Tbsp] unsalted butter, chilled and diced
a pinch of salt
100g [scant 1 cup] cream cheese
about 2 Tbsp ice-cold water
1 tsp lemon juice

Topping
150g [¾ cup] caster [granulated] sugar
50g [3½ Tbsp] unsalted butter
a pinch of sea salt flakes
10–12 Golden Delicious apples
crème fraîche, to serve

You will need a heavy-based skillet or ovenproof frying pan with a base measurement of 20cm [8in] and top measurement of 25cm [10in]

Serves 6 greedy or 8 not-so-greedy folk

Start by making the pastry so that it has plenty of resting time. Tip the flour into a bowl, add the diced butter and salt. Very lightly rub the butter into the flour, just enough to knock off the corners of the dice, then add the cream cheese in small spoonfuls. Mix gently to lightly combine and to coat the cream cheese in flour. Add the water and the lemon juice and mix with a round-bladed or palette knife to bring the dough together, adding more water if needed. Gather the dough together using your hands and shape into a neat square. Cover with cling film [plastic wrap] and chill for 1 hour.

Roll out the dough on a lightly floured surface into a neat rectangle that is three times as long as it is wide, with a thickness of about 5mm [¼in]. Fold the bottom third of the dough up into the middle and the top third down to cover it, to create a 3-layered square of dough. Turn this square 90° and roll out in the same way again. Fold the dough up as previously described, cover with cling film and chill for another hour.

Repeat this rolling and folding again so that you will have folded the dough 4 times in total. Cover with cling film and chill again for at least 1 hour before using.

Preheat the oven to 190°C/375°F/Gas 5.

continued »

continued »

Tip the sugar into the skillet or frying pan in an even layer and set the pan over a low heat to slowly melt the sugar, without stirring. Continue to cook the sugar until it starts to turn a rich amber-coloured caramel, gently swirling the pan to ensure that it caramelizes evenly. Add the butter and salt flakes to the caramel and gently stir to melt the butter into the caramel. Remove from the heat.

Peel, core and cut the apples in half. Arrange the apples cut side up in the skillet, starting from the outside and working towards the middle, packing the apples tightly side by side. Cover the skillet tightly with foil and bake on the middle shelf of the oven for 1 hour, turning the skillet around after 30 minutes so that the apples cook evenly. Carefully remove the foil – the apples will be hot and steamy and by now should be golden and tender.

Set the skillet over a medium–high heat and bubble to cook off a little of the caramel and apple syrup.

Roll out the pastry on a lightly floured surface into a neat round just slightly larger than the top of the apple skillet, and cut out using a dinner plate as a guide. Carefully lay the pastry on top of the apples, tucking in the edges rather like making a bed. Using a skewer, poke a hole in the middle of the pastry for steam to escape. Return the skillet or pan to the heat and cook for 1 minute until the pastry just starts to melt and bubble at the edges.

Slide the skillet back into the oven and cook for 40–45 minutes until the pastry is risen and deep golden brown. Leave to rest for about 5 minutes then lay a serving plate on top of the skillet. With your hands and arms protected by a cloth or oven glove, carefully turn the tart out onto the plate – the caramel will be hot, so take care.

Serve the tarte Tatin warm with tangy crème fraîche on the side.

TREACLE TART WITH GINGER & BOURBON

Where gingerbread and treacle tart meet…

Most of the elements of this dessert can be prepared partly or fully in advance. If you have a bottle of smoky bourbon in your cupboards then do use it here – if not, whisky would be a perfectly suitable substitute.

While we're talking about substitutions, black treacle is perhaps a distinctly British ingredient which might prove awkward to find elsewhere unless you happen to live near a well-stocked gourmet food store. You could use molasses at a push, or alternatively add the same quantity of dark brown sugar.

crystallized ginger, chopped,
  to decorate

Sweet pastry
250g [1¾ cups plus 2 Tbsp] plain
  [all-purpose] flour, plus extra
  for rolling out
a good pinch of salt
150g [²/₃ cup] unsalted butter,
  chilled and diced
40g [4½ Tbsp] icing
  [confectioners'] sugar
1 tsp ground mixed spice
2 medium egg yolks (keep 1 of the
  whites for sealing the pastry)
2 Tbsp ice-cold water
2 tsp lemon juice

ingredients continued »

Prepare the sweet pastry using the ingredients on this page and following the instructions on page 11. Add the mixed spice at the same time as the icing sugar. Chill for 1 hour or until firm.

Roll the dough out on a lightly floured surface into a neat round, about 2mm [¹/₁₆in] thick. Carefully line the tin with the pastry round and trim off any excess. (Any excess pastry/off-cuts can be used to make little stars or other shapes to decorate the tart.) Chill the pastry case for 20 minutes while you preheat the oven to 180°C/350°F/ Gas 4. Place a solid baking sheet on the middle shelf of the oven as it heats.

Prick the pastry base with a fork, line with foil and fill with baking rice. Place on top of the hot baking sheet and bake in the oven for about 15 minutes until crisp and pale golden. Remove the foil and rice and continue to cook for a further 5 minutes to dry out the bottom. Brush the base of the tart with lightly beaten egg white and return to the oven for 2 minutes – this will prevent the pastry bottom becoming soggy once the filling goes in.

continued »

continued »

Filling
250g [8¾oz] fresh brown
   breadcrumbs
finely grated zest of ½ lemon
325g [1 cup] golden syrup
75g [4 Tbsp] black treacle
75g [⅓ cup] double [heavy] cream
2 Tbsp bourbon (Maker's Mark)
2 large eggs plus 1 large yolk
2–3 nuggets of stem ginger in
   syrup, drained and chopped
   into smaller pieces
a large pinch sea salt flakes
   (smoked if you're so inclined),
   plus extra to sprinkle

You will need a 22-cm [8¾-in]
   fluted tart tin

Serves at least 8

Prepare the filling. Tip the breadcrumbs into a bowl, add the lemon zest, golden syrup, treacle, cream, bourbon, eggs and extra yolk, and mix well to thoroughly combine. Add the stem ginger to the mixture with the salt flakes. Mix again to combine and scoop into the baked pie shell. Spread level with a palette knife or the back of a spoon. Slide back into the oven and bake for 15 minutes and then spin the tart around, reduce the oven temperature to 150°C/300°F/Gas 2 and bake for a further 15–20 minutes until the filling has set.

Leave to cool down to warm or room temperature, then decorate with chopped crystallized ginger and sprinkle with sea salt. Serve with thick double cream, crème fraîche or vanilla ice cream.

APPLE & BLACKCURRANT SLAB PIE

I love the contrast between sweet, juicy apples, flaky buttery pastry and tart, lip-smacking blackcurrants – particularly when accompanied by ice cream. I've used blackcurrants here but you could use blueberries or blackberries – though they will be slightly sweeter so adjust the sugar accordingly. Serve this pie fresh from the oven or at room temperature.

Filling
4 crisp eating apples
2–3 Tbsp caster [granulated] sugar, plus extra for sprinkling
a squeeze of lemon juice
200g [7oz] blackcurrants

Sweet pastry
350g [2²/₃ cups] plain [all-purpose] flour, plus extra for rolling out
a good pinch of salt
225g [1 cup] unsalted butter, chilled and diced
50g [5¾ Tbsp] icing [confectioners'] sugar, sifted
1 medium egg yolk (save the white for glazing)
3–4 Tbsp ice-cold water
1 tsp lemon juice

You will need a 20 x 30-cm [8 x 12-in] baking tin

Makes 8–12 squares

Start by making the filling so that it has time to cool before assembling the pie. Peel, quarter, core and thinly slice the apples and tip into a medium-sized saucepan. Add 2 tablespoons of sugar and the lemon juice, cover the pan, set over a low-medium heat and cook for about 5 minutes, stirring from time to time until the apples soften but still retain some texture. Add the blackcurrants and return to the heat, uncovered, for a further 5 minutes or so, until the blackcurrants burst and the purée thickens slightly. Remove from the heat and leave to cool. Once cold, taste and add a little more sugar if it is a little on the tart side. Personally, I like the contrast of tart fruit and sweet flaky pastry so I tend to err on the side of tartness.

Prepare the sweet pastry using the ingredients on this page and following the instructions on page 11. Flatten into a rectangle, cover with cling film [plastic wrap] and chill for 1 hour or until firm.

Divide the dough in two, with one portion slightly larger than the other. On a lightly floured surface, roll out the larger piece into a rectangle and line the base and sides of the baking tin, allowing any extra to hang over the edges. Spoon the cooled apple mixture into the pastry case. Roll the second piece of pastry into a rectangle slightly larger than the top of the pie. Brush the edges with water and place on top of the filling, then press the edges together to seal, and trim off any excess with a sharp knife. Crimp the edges and chill for 20 minutes. Preheat the oven to 180°C/350°F/Gas 4, placing a solid baking sheet inside.

Brush the top of the pie with beaten egg white, sprinkle with sugar and snip holes into the pastry using scissors. Place on the hot baking sheet and bake for about 35 minutes, turning the sheet around halfway through, until the filling is piping hot and the pastry is crisp and golden. Cool slightly and serve with ice cream.

SWEET

M'HANNCHA

This Moroccan pastry is usually made using *warka* pastry – which is hard to find in shops outside of Morocco (or France) and even harder to make yourself. Filo is a good substitute, though it does require some careful and swift handling to avoid it cracking or drying out. Preparation is key – have your filling ready to go (not chilled) and an extra pair of hands on stand-by should you feel it necessary to draft in support when rolling your metre-long pastry.

170–200g [6–7oz] filo [phyllo] pastry
75g [⅓ cup] unsalted butter, melted
25g [⅓ cup] flaked [slivered] almonds
1–2 Tbsp clear honey
icing [confectioners'] sugar, for dusting
dried rose petals, to decorate

Filling
175g [1⅓ cups] almonds
75g [½ cup] pistachios
75g [⅓ cup] unsalted butter, softened
100g [½ cup] caster [granulated] sugar
1 medium egg, plus 1 medium yolk
50g [1¾oz] dried cherries, finely chopped
1 tsp finely grated lemon zest
1 tsp finely grated orange zest
1 tsp rosewater or orange blossom water
1 tsp ground cinnamon
1 Tbsp plain [all-purpose] flour
a good pinch of sea salt flakes

You will need a 20-cm [8-in] springform tin, base unclipped from the sides

Serves 8

Preheat the oven to 180°C/350°F/Gas 4.

To make the filling, tip the almonds and pistachios into a food processor and blend until very finely chopped – stop whizzing before the nuts become dust or butter. In a bowl and using a spatula or wooden spoon, cream the softened butter with the sugar. Add the whole egg and extra yolk and mix again to combine. Tip the nuts into the bowl along with the finely chopped dried cherries, lemon and orange zests, rosewater or orange blossom water, cinnamon, flour and salt. Mix to combine, scoop into a disposable piping [pastry] bag, snip the end into a 1.5–2-cm [½–¾-in] wide nozzle, and set aside.

Working quickly, cut the filo pastry sheets into long strips each 16cm [6½in] wide (the brand that I use is 32 x 40cm/13 x 16in so I cut each sheet in half to give two long strips 40cm/16in long x 16cm/6½in wide).

Lay two clean tea towels horizontally on the work surface, overlapping slightly so that they cover a length of just over 1 metre [3 feet]. Lay one sheet of filo horizontally at the right hand end of the tea towels, with the long edge closest to you, and brush with melted butter. Lay a second sheet of filo alongside to the left and overlapping by 4cm [1½in]. Brush this sheet with butter and lay a third sheet, again overlapping on the left hand side by 4cm [1½in]. By now you should have a long strip of buttered filo that is 1 metre [3 feet] long and 16cm [6½in] wide. Place another layer of filo sheets on top, brush with butter and repeat. By now, you will have a stack of 3 layers of buttered filo pastry, 1 metre [3 feet] long.

continued »

continued »

Pipe the nut filling in a long sausage along
the bottom edge of the pastry, leaving
a 1–2-cm [³/₈–¾-in] border at each end.
Using the tea towel to support the pastry
(and drafting in another pair of hands if
necessary) roll the pastry up and over into
a long snake, with the filling completely
encased in filo and finishing with the
join on the underside. Fold one end
underneath to seal the filling inside and
roll the pastry snake into a flat coil, using
your hands to support the pastry and
prevent the filo cracking. Carefully slide
the coil onto the springform base and tuck
the tail end of the pastry underneath to
prevent the filling oozing out.

Clip the cake tin sides together, brush
the pastry with melted butter and patch
up any cracks with scraps of buttered
filo 'bandages'. Sprinkle over the flaked
almonds and bake on the middle shelf of
the oven for 45 minutes until the pastry is
crisp and golden, turning the tin around
halfway through baking to ensure that it
cooks evenly.

Remove from the oven, warm the honey,
brush over the top of the m'hanncha and
leave to cool.

Serve at room temperature, dusted with
icing sugar and decorated with dried rose
petals, cut into wedges.

TARTE FINE

It's staggering how good just a few ingredients can be when prepared carefully. However – and here's the rub – homemade puff pastry will take this tart to the next level. And when something is this easy to make you owe it to yourself to at least make the pastry… For the best results you really do need to slice the apples using a mandolin – that way they will be of uniform thickness, easier to arrange and will cook evenly. And the overall look of the finished tart will be so much more professional.

continued »

400g [14oz] puff pastry
(see page 12 for homemade)
plain [all-purpose] flour,
for rolling out
1 Tbsp ground almonds
2 Tbsp caster [granulated] sugar
6 crisp dessert apples, such as
Braeburn, Golden Delicious or
Granny Smith
1–2 Tbsp melted unsalted butter
2 Tbsp apricot jam
1 tsp lemon juice

Serves 8

Roll out the pastry on a floured surface into a neat circle. Using a plate or cake tin as a guide, cut the pastry into a 25-cm [10-in] round. Carefully transfer the pastry to a baking sheet lined with baking parchment and use a sharp knife to knock up the pastry edges (see page 135).

Chill for 30 minutes while you prepare the apple topping and preheat the oven to 220°C/425°F/Gas 7, placing a solid baking sheet on the middle shelf to heat up.

Peel the apples and remove the core, using a corer. Slice the apples into thin, neat rings using a mandolin, stacking each apple back into slices.

Sprinkle the ground almonds and half the sugar over the pastry. Arrange the apple slices in neat, close, overlapping circles on top of the almonds – starting at the outside edge of the pastry round and working towards the middle.

Generously brush the apples with the melted butter and sprinkle over the remaining sugar. Place on the hot baking sheet and bake in the oven for 25 minutes then turn the sheet around and reduce the heat to 200°C/400°F/Gas 6. Continue to cook for a further 15 minutes until the apples are starting to caramelize at the edges.

Melt the apricot jam with the lemon juice, strain into a bowl and brush over the top of the apples. Leave to cool to room temperature to serve.

CHERRY & ALMOND SOURDOUGH PIE

For this recipe you will need a starter that is at 100% hydration, i.e. one that has been fed an equal weight of flour to water.

This pastry needs a little advance planning. Not only does the sourdough starter need to be fed but it needs to be chilled too. And for best results I recommend making the pastry the day before you plan on using it.

Sourdough pastry
175g [1⅓ cups] plain [all-purpose] flour, plus extra for rolling out
1 Tbsp caster [granulated] sugar
a good pinch of salt
150g [⅔ cup] unsalted butter, chilled and diced
175g [6¼oz] active starter (100% hydration), chilled
1 Tbsp milk or a beaten egg, for glazing

Filling
750g [scant 1¾lb] dark cherries
2 Tbsp golden caster [granulated] sugar, plus extra for sprinkling
1½ Tbsp cornflour [cornstarch]
juice of ½ lemon
1 tsp vanilla bean paste
75g [2¾oz] marzipan, broken into nuggets

You will need a 20–22-cm [8–8¾-in] pie dish, 5cm [2in] deep

Serves 6–8

Prepare the sourdough pastry following the instructions on page 14 and leave to rest overnight.

To make the filling, stone the cherries using a cherry stoner – do this over a bowl to catch the cherry juice, and preferably not wearing your best white shirt. Add the sugar, cornflour, lemon juice and vanilla to the cherries and mix well to combine.

Divide the sourdough pastry in two, with one portion slightly larger than the other. Roll out the larger piece on a lightly floured work surface to a round about 3mm [⅛in] thick and use to line the pie dish, allowing any excess pastry to drape over the sides. Scoop half the cherries into the pastry case and sprinkle over half the marzipan. Spoon over the remaining cherries and all of the juices left in the bowl, followed by the rest of the marzipan.

Roll the second piece of pastry out into a round that is comfortably larger than the top of the pie. Cut the pastry into strips of varying widths. Arrange the strips randomly on top of the cherries. Trim any excess pastry from the sides and press a fork into the rim of the pie to seal the edges together. Chill for 20 minutes while you preheat the oven to 180°C/350°F/Gas 4, placing a solid baking sheet inside to heat up.

Brush the lattice with milk or beaten egg and sprinkle with sugar. Place on the hot baking sheet and bake for 15 minutes, then reduce the oven temperature to 170°C/330°F/Gas 3½ and bake for a further 35 minutes until the pastry is deep golden brown and the cherries are bubbling and tender. Loosely cover the pie with foil if it's browning too quickly. Serve hot, warm or at room temperature with cream or ice cream.

RHUBARB & CUSTARD TART

It has become something of a cliché to pair rhubarb with custard, but it's a cliché for a good reason. Poached or baked rhubarb comes alive when served with vanilla or spice-scented custard. Save making this tart for when forced pink rhubarb is in season to make the most of its fabulous colour. By good fortune, blood oranges should be in plentiful supply at the same time, giving you a double hit of colour.

continued »

500g [1lb 2oz] tender-stemmed, forced rhubarb
2 Tbsp caster [granulated] sugar
juice of 1 blood orange
2 star anise
½ vanilla pod [bean], split in half lengthways
500g [1lb 2oz] all-butter puff pastry (see page 12 for homemade)
plain [all-purpose] flour, for rolling out
1 egg, beaten, for glazing
icing [confectioners'] sugar, for dusting

Custard
300ml [1¼ cups] whole milk
½ vanilla pod [bean], split in half lengthways
4 medium egg yolks
75g [6 Tbsp] caster [granulated] sugar
1 Tbsp cornflour [cornstarch]

Serves 6

To make the custard, heat the milk with the vanilla pod in a small pan over a low heat. Remove the pan from the heat just before the milk boils and leave to infuse for 15 minutes. In a medium bowl, whisk together the egg yolks, sugar and cornflour. Remove the pod from the milk, re-heat the milk until just below boiling point and, whisking constantly, pour the hot milk onto the egg mixture. Whisk until smooth and combined, return to the pan and, stirring constantly, cook over a low–medium heat until just boiling and the custard starts to thicken. You should not be able to taste any cornflour – if you can, cook for a further 20 seconds until it has cooked out and the custard is glossy, thickened and smooth. Strain into a clean bowl, cover the surface with cling film [plastic wrap] to prevent a skin forming and leave until cold. Chill until needed.

Preheat the oven to 180°C/350°F/Gas 4. Trim the rhubarb, cut into 7.5-cm [3-in] lengths, tip into a bowl and add the sugar, orange juice, star anise and split vanilla pod. Mix well to combine. Tip into a ceramic or non-reactive ovenproof dish in a single layer and bake on the middle shelf for 10–15 minutes until the rhubarb is juicy and just tender when tested with a knife. Leave to cool.

Roll the pastry out on a floured surface into a 30 x 25-cm [12 x 10-in] rectangle. Cut a 1.5-cm [½-in] strip from all four sides and place the pastry rectangle on a baking sheet lined with baking parchment. Brush the edges with water and place the strips on top to create a border. Chill for 30 minutes. Preheat the oven to 190°C/375°F/Gas 5. Prick the base of the pastry with a fork, knock up the outside edges with a knife (see page 135) and brush the border with beaten egg. Bake on the middle shelf for 15 minutes until the frame is golden and the base risen and golden. Cool for 10 minutes, then spread the custard over the base. Arrange the roasted rhubarb on top, reserving any juices, and return the tart to the oven for 25–30 minutes until the pastry is golden brown and crisp, the custard set and the rhubarb starting to caramelize at the edges.

Tip any rhubarb pan juices into a small pan, bring to the boil and reduce until slightly thickened. Leave the tart to cool, then drizzle with the reduced rhubarb juices.

BUTTERMILK CUSTARD TART WITH ROASTED GRAPES

I like to serve this creamy, vanilla-scented tart with roasted grapes, but you could also serve it with roasted figs or summer berries macerated in lemon juice and sugar.

Pâte sablée

100g [½ cup minus 1 Tbsp] unsalted butter, at room temperature

50g [5¾ Tbsp] icing [confectioners'] sugar, plus extra for dusting

2 medium egg yolks (save 1 egg white for sealing the pastry)

1 tsp vanilla extract

175g [1⅓ cups] plain [all-purpose] flour, plus extra for rolling out

a pinch of salt

1 Tbsp double [heavy] cream

Buttermilk custard

250ml [generous 1 cup] double [heavy] cream

2 bay leaves

1 vanilla pod [bean], split in half lengthways

3 pared strips of lemon zest

4 medium eggs, plus 2 medium yolks

100g [½ cup] caster [granulated] sugar

285ml [scant 1¼ cups] buttermilk

a pinch of salt

Roasted grapes

400-g [14-oz] bunch of seedless black grapes, still on the stalk

2 Tbsp Marsala

1 Tbsp hazelnut oil (or olive oil)

juice of ¼ lemon

1 Tbsp caster [granulated] sugar

You will need a 21-cm [8-in] straight-sided tart ring

Serves 8

Prepare the pâte sablée following the instructions on page 13 and chill for at least 1 hour or until firm. Meanwhile, prepare the buttermilk custard. Pour the cream into a small pan and add the bay leaves. Scoop the seeds from the vanilla pod into the pan and drop in the pod itself and the strips of lemon zest. Set the pan over a low–medium heat and bring to just below boiling point. Remove from the heat and leave to infuse for 1 hour.

Break the eggs and extra yolks into a bowl, add the sugar and whisk until smooth. Add the buttermilk, the infused cream and salt and whisk again until smooth. Cover and set aside or chill until ready to use.

Place the tart ring on a baking sheet lined with baking parchment. Roll the pastry out on a floured work surface into a neat round about 3mm [⅛in] thick. Line the tart ring, pushing the pastry neatly into the corners. Trim off the excess pastry with a sharp knife and chill the pastry case for at least 20 minutes while you preheat the oven to 170°C/330°F/Gas 3½. Prick the base of the tart case with a fork, line with foil and fill with baking rice. Bake on the middle shelf for about 15 minutes until pale golden along the top edges. Remove the foil and rice and bake for another couple of minutes to dry out the base. Brush the base with lightly beaten egg white and return to the oven for a further couple of minutes. Reduce the oven temperature to 150°C/300°F/Gas 2.

Strain the custard into the tart shell and bake for 30–35 minutes until the custard is just set, with the faintest wobble. Remove from the oven, leave to cool, then chill for an hour or so. Meanwhile, preheat the oven to 200°C/400°F/Gas 6 and put the grapes on a baking sheet. Drizzle with the Marsala, hazelnut oil and lemon juice, and sprinkle over the sugar. Bake on the middle shelf for 20 minutes until juicy and starting to burst. Remove from the oven and cool slightly. To serve, dust with icing sugar and top with the grapes and roasting juices.

APPLE & SALTED CARAMEL PIE

This is the pie of the moment – all the fashionable places, cooks and cookbooks have a recipe for an old-style apple pie slathered in salted caramel and topped with all manner of intricate, fancy pastry lattice. And – not to be left out – here is my version. Using a combination of sweet and sharp tasting apples gives a good contrast to the caramel sauce. Tangy crème fraîche in my opinion is a perfect accompaniment, or failing that some stonkingly good vanilla ice cream.

Sweet pastry with rye

250g [1¾ cups plus 2 Tbsp] plain [all-purpose] flour, plus extra for rolling out

50g [6 Tbsp] white rye flour

a good pinch of salt

175g [¾ cup plus 1 tsp] unsalted butter, chilled and diced

2 Tbsp golden caster [granulated] sugar

1 medium egg yolk (save the white for glazing)

1 Tbsp cider vinegar

2½ Tbsp ice-cold water

milk, for brushing

Salted caramel

50g [¼ cup] caster [granulated] sugar

1 Tbsp hot water

75g [⅓ cup] double [heavy] cream

50g [¼ cup] light muscovado sugar

25g [1¾ Tbsp] unsalted butter

½ tsp vanilla bean paste

a pinch of sea salt flakes

Filling

about 1.25kg [2¾lb] apples – an equal mix of tart Bramleys and crisp, sweet eaters such as Braeburns

1½ Tbsp golden caster [granulated] sugar, plus extra for sprinkling

1 Tbsp cornflour [cornstarch]

juice of ½ lemon

4 cloves

1 tsp ground cinnamon

a grating of nutmeg

You will need a round pie dish with a base measurement of 20cm [8in]

Serves 8

Prepare the sweet pastry using the ingredients on this page and following the instructions on page 11, adding the rye flour at the same time as the plain flour. Chill for at least 1 hour until firm.

To make the salted caramel, put the caster sugar and water in a small saucepan. Set over a low–medium heat to dissolve the sugar without stirring. Bring to the boil and continue to cook until it turns into an amber-coloured caramel. Slide the pan off the heat, add the cream, muscovado sugar, butter, vanilla and salt. Return the pan to a low heat to re-melt the caramel and gently bubble, stirring constantly, until smooth. Pour into a bowl and leave until cold.

Divide the pastry in half, with one portion slightly larger than the other. Roll the larger piece out on a floured surface into a disc that is larger than the pie dish by about 5cm [2in] all round. Carefully line the pie dish, allowing the excess pastry to hang over the edges.

To make the filling, peel, core and thinly slice the apples. Tip the slices into a large bowl with the sugar, cornflour, lemon juice, cloves, cinnamon and nutmeg and mix well. Scoop one-third of the mixture into the pastry-lined pie and top with one-third of the caramel sauce. Repeat this layering, very slightly mounding the apples up in the middle for the last layer.

Take the remaining pastry and roll out into a neat disc, about 2–3mm [¹/₁₆–¹/₈in] thick and with a diameter at least 5cm [2in] wider than the top of the pie dish. Using a ruler and a pizza or pastry wheel – or a knife if that's what you prefer – cut the pastry into neat strips. Carefully pick one of the longest middle strips and lay it across the middle of the apple-filled pie, from top to bottom (vertically). Lay 2 slightly shorter strips either side of this. Taking another of the longest strips, lay it across the middle (horizontally), picking up the horizontal strips numbered one and three to lie underneath. Repeat this on either side horizontally, but this time picking up strip number 2 to lie underneath.

SWEET

continued »

continued »

Make sure that you keep the lattice even, neat and the strips lying close together. Repeat this lattice, alternating with horizontal and vertical strips and keeping the over and under strips even.

When the whole of the pie is covered, carefully lift up the strips on the edges, brush the edge of the pie with milk and press the lattice strips to seal. Using a sharp knife, trim off any excess pastry and use your fingers to crimp the edges decoratively.

Chill the pie for 30 minutes while you preheat the oven to 190°C/375°F/Gas 5, placing a solid baking sheet on the middle shelf to heat up.

Brush the top of the pie with lightly beaten egg white, sprinkle with sugar and cook on the hot baking sheet for 30 minutes, then turn the pie around, turn the oven down to 170°C/330°F/Gas 3½ and cook for a further 25–30 minutes until the pastry is deep golden and the apples are bubbling and tender when tested with a skewer. Leave to cool slightly, then serve with crème fraîche or ice cream.

PUMPKIN PIE WITH RYE & BOURBON

You may have realized that I don't like cutting corners so rather than opening a can of pumpkin purée, I have given you the option of making your own. Canned purée is not readily available in the UK all year round so some of you will be wanting (and needing) to make your own. Incidentally, I came across maple sugar on my travels in the baking aisle and am always looking for ways to use it; this pastry is one of those ways.

If you have maple leaf pastry cutters then use them to make decorations to adorn the pie. Free-form, hand-cut leaves are also mighty fine.

Brown sugar & rye pastry

150g [1 cup plus 2 Tbsp] plain [all-purpose] flour, plus extra for rolling out

100g [¾ cup] white rye flour

a good pinch of sea salt flakes

150g [⅔ cup] unsalted butter, diced and chilled

4 Tbsp maple sugar or soft light brown sugar

2 medium egg yolks

2 Tbsp ice-cold water

2 tsp cider vinegar or lemon juice

Filling

1.4–1.5kg [3–3¼lb] pumpkin or squash

75g [6 Tbsp] soft dark brown sugar

2 Tbsp bourbon

2 medium eggs, plus 2 medium egg yolks (reserve 1 egg white for glazing)

2 Tbsp maple syrup

100ml [⅓ cup plus 1 Tbsp] double [heavy] cream

1 tsp vanilla bean paste

½ tsp ground cinnamon

a good pinch each of ground allspice, cloves and nutmeg

a pinch of sea salt flakes

2 tsp caster [granulated] sugar

2 Tbsp pumpkin seeds

You will need a pie dish with a base measurement of 20cm [8in] and 4cm [1½in] deep

Serves 8–10

To make the brown sugar and rye pastry, tip both flours into a large mixing bowl and add the salt. Add the chilled, diced butter and, using a round-bladed or palette knife, cut the butter into the flour until the butter pieces are half their original size. Switch to using your hands to continue rubbing in until there are only small flecks of butter visible. Add the sugar and mix to combine.

Make a well in the middle of the mixture, add the egg yolks, cold water and vinegar and mix again using the palette knife until the pastry starts to clump together. Use your hands to gather the pastry into a neat ball and very gently knead for 20 seconds until smooth. Flatten the pastry into a disc, wrap in cling film [plastic wrap] and chill for at least 2 hours.

To make the filling, peel the pumpkin, cut the flesh into large chunks and discard the seeds. Tip the pumpkin pieces into a steamer, cover and cook over a pan of simmering water for about 30 minutes until tender when tested with the point of a knife. Keep an eye on the water level below the steamer basket and top up if necessary. Remove the pumpkin from the steamer basket and leave to cool and drain on a double layer of kitchen paper [paper towels].

Dust the work surface with flour, set aside 150g [5¼oz] of the pastry and roll out the remainder into a round, 3mm [⅛in] thick. Carefully line the pie dish with the pastry,

continued »

pressing it into the corners and trimming off any excess from the top. Crimp the edges into a decorative pattern and chill the pastry case for 30 minutes. Roll the reserved portion of pastry to a thickness of 2mm [$^1/_{16}$in] and cut into 3–4-cm [1¼–1½-in] leaf shapes. Gather any off-cuts and scraps and re-roll and stamp out more leaves.

Preheat the oven to 180°C/350°F/Gas 4 and place a solid baking sheet on the middle shelf to heat up.

Tip the cooked, cooled pumpkin into a food processor and blend until smooth. Weigh the purée – you will need 500g [1lb 2oz] (any left over can be turned into soup).

In a large bowl, whisk the dark brown sugar with the bourbon to dissolve any lumps. Add the whole eggs, extra yolks, maple syrup, cream, vanilla and spices and whisk to combine. Add the sea salt flakes and the cooled pumpkin purée and whisk again until smooth.

Pour the pumpkin filling into the chilled pastry case, brush the top edge of the pastry with a little water and arrange the pastry leaves on top. Lightly whisk the reserved egg white with a fork, brush over the leaves and sprinkle with caster sugar. Sprinkle the pumpkin seeds around the top of the pie and carefully slide into the oven on top of the hot baking sheet.

Cook for 20 minutes and then turn the oven down to 170°C/330°F/Gas 3½ and cook for another 15–20 minutes until the pastry is golden brown and the filling set, with the slightest wobble in the middle.

Leave the pie to cool to room temperature and serve with ice cream or crème fraîche.

SWEET

LEMON & ALMOND TART

I love this tart for its elegance that belies its simplicity. It uses one food processor bowl, one pan and does away with the need for a rolling pin. Pastry-phobes rejoice! As this recipe is so simple you could go to town on the decoration and make some candied lemon zest to scatter over the top – or you could just sit back and enjoy.

Pastry
175g [1⅓ cups] plain [all-purpose] flour
40g [½ cup] flaked [slivered] almonds
1½ Tbsp caster [granulated] sugar
a pinch of salt
125g [½ cup plus 1 Tbsp] unsalted butter, chilled and diced
1 Tbsp ice-cold water

Filling
5 medium eggs
200g [generous 1 cup] caster [granulated] sugar
finely grated zest and juice of 2 large lemons
40g [3 Tbsp] unsalted butter, diced
50g [generous ½ cup] flaked [slivered] almonds
icing [confectioners'] sugar, for dusting

You will need a 35 x 11-cm [14 x 4½-in] rectangular tart tin with a removable base

Serves 6–8

To make the pastry, tip the flour into the bowl of a food processor, add the flaked almonds, sugar and salt and pulse until the almonds are finely chopped. Add the diced butter and pulse again to rub the butter into the dry ingredients. Add the cold water and pulse again to combine, stopping when the dough starts to clump together into little nuggets.

Using your fingers, press the crumbly, buttery dough into the tart tin, evenly covering the base and sides. Chill the base for 20 minutes while you preheat the oven to 180°C/350°F/Gas 4, placing a solid baking sheet on the middle shelf of the oven to heat up.

Bake the base on the hot baking sheet for 20–25 minutes until pale golden all over. Remove from the oven and increase the temperature to 190°C/375°F/Gas 5.

While the pastry is cooking, prepare the filling. Crack the eggs into a medium saucepan and add the sugar, lemon zest and juice. Whisk until smooth then place over a low heat and cook, stirring constantly, until the mixture thickens and will coat the back of a spoon. Do not allow it to boil or the eggs will scramble. Remove from the heat, scoop into a bowl and add the butter. Whisk to combine and set aside to cool for 20 minutes.

Spoon the curd into the baked pastry shell, sprinkle the flaked almonds around the edges and return to the oven for a further 10–15 minutes until the almonds are golden and the filling is lightly burnished and puffed up.

Leave to cool and then dust with icing sugar and cut into fingers to serve.

103

APRICOT & ALMOND CROSTATA

Essentially this is a large jam tart – with extras. I've added crushed amaretti to the dough, which is an idea I read about and have fiddled with – though I just cannot remember where I read it, so apologies to whomever it was for not crediting you. The biscuits should be crushed with a rolling pin rather than in a food processor so that they retain texture. They add a delicious crunch and marzipan taste to the dough.

1 x 370-g [13-oz] jar good-quality
    apricot jam
25g [⅓ cup] flaked [slivered]
    almonds
icing [confectioners'] sugar,
    for dusting (optional)

Crostata dough
75g [2¾oz] crisp amaretti biscuits
250g [1¾ cups plus 2 Tbsp] plain
    [all-purpose] flour, plus extra
    for rolling out
a pinch of salt
175g [¾ cup plus 1 tsp] unsalted
    butter, chilled and diced
1 Tbsp caster [granulated] sugar,
    plus extra for sprinkling
1 tsp finely grated lemon zest
1 medium egg, plus 1 medium
    yolk (save the white for glazing)
1 Tbsp ice-cold water
1 tsp lemon juice

You will need a 22-cm [8¾-in]
    fluted tart tin with a removable
    base

Serves 8–10

To make the crostata dough, tip the amaretti into a freezer bag, twist the end to seal and bash with a rolling pin to reduce the biscuits to crumbs. Put the flour and salt into a large mixing bowl, add the butter and rub into the dry ingredients using your fingertips. Add the crushed amaretti, sugar and lemon zest and mix to combine.

Make a well in the middle of the mixture and add the whole egg, extra yolk, water and lemon juice. Use a round-bladed or palette knife to bring the dough together – it will be quite sticky – gather into a ball, flatten into a disc, cover with cling film [plastic wrap] and chill for about 2 hours or until firm.

Cut off one-third of the dough and keep it chilled. Roll the remaining two-thirds of the dough out on a lightly floured surface into a neat round, 2cm [¾in] larger all round than the tart tin. Carefully line the tin, pressing the dough into the corners and ridges, then trim off any excess pastry from the top. Spoon the jam into the crostata shell and spread evenly with the back of a spoon. Roll out the remaining pastry, with any off-cuts, into a round slightly larger than the top of the tart tin. Cut the dough into 1-cm [⅜-in] wide strips using a pizza wheel or long knife. Arrange the dough strips in a neat lattice on top of the jam-filled tart, leaving a gap of about 1cm [⅜in] between each strip. Press the lattice to the sides of the tart shell to stick, trim the top edge to neaten and chill for 20 minutes. Meanwhile, preheat the oven to 180°C/350°F/ Gas 4 and place a solid baking sheet on the middle shelf of the oven to heat up.

Brush the lattice and edges with lightly beaten egg white, sprinkle with sugar and flaked almonds, place on the hot baking sheet and bake for about 35 minutes. Leave to cool to room temperature to serve.

QUINCE, TAHINI & ALMOND TART

I have a thing about quince, so much so that we planted a tree in our garden which has yet to produce any fruit of quality or quantity – but I live in hope. Quince blossoms are delicate white petals that are beautifully scented – as are the fruit, which will perfume your kitchen as they sit in the fruit bowl.

Tahini makes a wonderful addition to frangipane – adding a warming note that pairs beautifully with the quince. If quince prove hard to track down or are out of season, you could use plums, apricots or pears here.

Poached quince
600ml [2½ cups] water
200g [1 cup] caster [granulated] sugar
juice of 1 lemon
2 star anise
1 vanilla pod [bean], split in half lengthways
2 large quince (or 4 small)

Sweet pastry
200g [1½ cups] plain [all-purpose] flour, plus extra for rolling out
a good pinch of salt
125g [½ cup plus 1 Tbsp] unsalted butter, chilled and diced
1 Tbsp icing [confectioners'] sugar, sifted
1 medium egg yolk
2 Tbsp ice-cold water
1 tsp lemon juice

ingredients continued »

For the poached quince, pour the water into a medium saucepan, add the sugar, lemon juice, star anise and halved vanilla pod. Peel the quince, cut into quarters and drop into the pan – do not worry about removing the cores at this stage. The fruit should fit snugly in the pan and be just covered by the syrup – top up with a little more water if necessary. Place the pan over a medium heat and bring slowly to the boil to dissolve the sugar. Cover the fruit with a circle of baking parchment and simmer gently for about 25 minutes until tender when tested with the point of a knife. Remove from the heat and leave to cool in the syrup.

Meanwhile, prepare the sweet pastry using the ingredients on this page and following the instructions on page 11. Chill for at least 1 hour.

Roll the dough out on a lightly floured surface to a neat round, 2–3mm [¹⁄₁₆–¹⁄₈in] thick and with a diameter that is 3–4cm [1¼–1½in] wider all round than the tart ring. Line the tart ring, pressing the pastry neatly into the corners and allowing any excess to drape over the sides. Prick the base with a fork and chill for 30 minutes while you preheat the oven to 180°C/350°F/Gas 4, placing a solid baking sheet on the middle shelf to heat up.

Line the cold pastry case with foil, pressing it neatly into the corners, fill with baking rice and bake for 20 minutes until the sides and edges are pale golden. Remove the foil and rice and bake for a further 5 minutes to dry

continued »

Tahini frangipane
100g [½ cup minus 1 Tbsp]
   unsalted butter, softened
100g [½ cup] caster [granulated]
   sugar
2 medium egg yolks
100g [scant ½ cup] tahini
75g [¾ cup] ground almonds
1 Tbsp crème fraîche
1 tsp finely grated lemon zest
a pinch of sea salt flakes

You will need a 25-cm [10-in]
   tart ring or tin

Serves 8

out the base. Leave to cool while you prepare the tahini frangipane and quince.

Beat the softened butter and sugar until thoroughly combined, add the egg yolks and beat again. Add the tahini, ground almonds, crème fraîche, lemon zest and salt and mix again until smooth. Drain the quince from the poaching liquid and carefully remove the core and seeds. Thinly slice the quince.

Spread the frangipane into the tart shell, evenly covering the base, and arrange the quince slices, slightly overlapping, all over the frangipane. Place the tart on the hot baking sheet and bake for 45–50 minutes until the pastry is crisp, the frangipane is golden and the quince slices are starting to caramelize at the edges.

Leave to cool to room temperature and serve with crème fraîche.

SWEET

PLUM & BLACKBERRY CRUMBLE PIE

Who says you can't have it all? If you can't make your mind up whether
to go for pie or crumble – have both. A buttery, crisp pastry shell, filled
with juicy, slightly jammy fruit and topped with a nutty crumble – pass
me a spoon! This has Sunday lunch written all over it.

Sweet pastry
200g [1½ cups] plain [all-purpose]
    flour, plus extra for rolling out
a pinch of salt
125g [½ cup plus 1 Tbsp] unsalted
    butter
40g [4½ Tbsp] icing
    [confectioners'] sugar, sifted
1 medium egg yolk
2–3 Tbsp ice-cold water
1 tsp lemon juice

Filling
450g [1lb] plums
150g [5¼oz] blackberries
2 Tbsp light muscovado sugar
1 tsp vanilla bean paste
juice of ½ lemon
1 Tbsp cornflour [cornstarch]

Crumble
40g [3¼ Tbsp] light muscovado
    sugar
40g [4¾ Tbsp] plain [all-purpose]
    flour
40g [3 Tbsp] unsalted butter,
    chilled and diced
½ tsp ground cinnamon
a pinch of salt
40g [⅓ cup] hazelnuts, very
    roughly chopped

You will need a 20-cm [8-in]
    round pie dish

Serves 6–8

Prepare the sweet pastry following the instructions on
page 11 and chill for at least 1 hour until firm.

Roll out the dough on a lightly floured surface into a neat
disc, 3–4mm [⅛in] thick, with a diameter of about 25cm
[10in]. Line the pie dish with the pastry, press it into the
corners, trim any excess from the top and crimp the
top pastry edge between your fingers. Chill for at least
30 minutes while you prepare the filling and preheat the
oven to 190°C/375°F/Gas 5. Place a solid baking sheet
on the middle shelf to heat up at the same time.

Quarter the plums, remove the stones and tip into a large
bowl. Add the blackberries, sugar, vanilla, lemon juice and
cornflour, mix well to combine and set aside while you
prepare the crumble.

Tip the sugar, flour and diced butter into a bowl, add
the cinnamon and salt and rub the butter into the dry
ingredients until the crumble starts to clump together in
little nuggets. Add the hazelnuts and mix to combine.

Scoop the fruit mixture and all of the sugary juice into
the chilled pie crust and spread in an even layer. Sprinkle
the crumble over the top, slide the pie into the oven onto
the hot baking sheet and bake for 10 minutes. Reduce the
oven temperature to 170°C/330°F/Gas 3½ and continue
cooking for a further 35–40 minutes until the pastry is
golden, the fruit is bubbling and the crumble is crisp.

Leave to cool for 5 minutes then serve hot, warm or at
room temperature.

RUFFLED MILK PIE

This pie bears a passing resemblance to bread and butter pudding.
Buttery layers of pastry are baked in a lightly spiced, egg-rich custard.
I've added a handful of plump sultanas, candied peel and crisp nuts to
give this ruffled pie a hint of sophistication.

250g [8¾oz] (about 10 sheets) filo
  [phyllo] pastry
75g [⅓ cup] unsalted butter,
  melted
400ml [1⅔ cups] whole milk
1 tsp anise seeds
4 medium eggs, plus 1 medium
  yolk
50g [¼ cup] caster [granulated]
  sugar
2 Tbsp clear, fragrant honey
100ml [⅓ cup plus 1 Tbsp] double
  [heavy] cream
½ tsp ground cinnamon
finely grated zest of ½ lemon
1 tsp finely grated orange zest
½ tsp vanilla bean paste
a pinch of salt
75g [½ cup] sultanas [golden
  raisins]
30g [scant ¼ cup] candied peel
30g [⅓ cup] flaked [slivered]
  almonds
30g [1oz] nibbed pistachios
icing [confectioners'] sugar,
  for dusting

You will need a 20-cm [8-in]
  solid-bottomed, deep pie dish

Serves 8

Preheat the oven to 180°C/350°F/Gas 4.

Unwrap the filo pastry and cover with a very slightly
damp, clean tea towel. Take the first sheet of filo, brush
with melted butter to cover completely and fold the
pastry into 3–4-cm [1¼–1½-in] pleats, concertina style,
starting with one of the longer sides. Repeat until you
have buttered and pleated each sheet. Gather each pastry
strip into ruffles and arrange upright in the dish, filling
it evenly. Place the dish on a solid baking sheet and bake
on the middle shelf of the oven for about 20 minutes until
the pastry is crisp and golden. Reduce the temperature
to 150°C/300°F/Gas 2.

Meanwhile, prepare the filling. Heat the milk in a
small saucepan with the anise seeds and bring slowly
to the boil. Remove from the heat and leave to infuse
for 30 minutes.

Break the eggs and yolk into a bowl, add the sugar and
honey and whisk to combine. Add the cream, cinnamon,
lemon and orange zest, vanilla and salt. Add the infused
milk and whisk to combine.

Sprinkle the sultanas and candied peel over the filo and
pour over the custard mixture. Slide the pie back into
the oven and cook for 20 minutes then sprinkle over the
flaked almonds and nibbed pistachios and continue to
cook for a further 10–15 minutes, until the top is browned
and the custard set.

Leave to cool to room temperature and dust with icing
sugar to serve.

APRICOT, HONEY
& LABNEH SHORTBREAD

Labneh is strained yogurt that couldn't be easier to make and can be
used in many ways – both sweet and savoury – often in place of cream
cheese. I particularly like using sheep's milk yogurt for its mild yet
creamy flavour. It is an especially delicious partner for honey-roasted
apricots. If you don't like it, just use a good-quality Greek yogurt.

Sweet labneh
500g/2 cups sheep's milk yogurt
a pinch of salt
1–2 Tbsp clear honey, to taste
1 tsp finely grated lemon zest

Shortbread
125g [½ cup plus 1 Tbsp] unsalted
   butter, softened
75g [6 Tbsp] caster [granulated]
   sugar
1 medium egg yolk
1 tsp finely grated lemon zest
150g [1 cup plus 2 Tbsp] plain
   [all-purpose] flour
50g [½ cup] cornflour
   [cornstarch], rice flour
   or semolina
a pinch of sea salt flakes

Topping
10–12 fresh apricots, halved
   and stoned
3 pared strips of lemon zest
1 vanilla pod [bean], halved
1 sprig of thyme
3 Tbsp lemon juice
3 Tbsp clear honey
1 Tbsp water
100g [¾ cup] blueberries
40g [1½oz] nibbed pistachios

To decorate (optional)
bee pollen
edible flowers

You will need a 35 x 11-cm
   [14 x 4½-in] rectangular tart
   tin with a removable base

Serves 6–8

Prepare the sweet labneh the night before. Stir the salt
into the yogurt then scoop the yogurt into a sieve lined
with a new, clean J-cloth or muslin [cheesecloth]. Set the
sieve over a bowl, cover with cling film [plastic wrap] and
refrigerate for 24 hours to allow the whey to drain off.

To make the shortbread base, cream together the butter
and sugar until pale and light. Add the egg yolk and
lemon zest and beat to combine. Add the flour, cornflour
and sea salt and mix again using a rubber spatula until the
shortbread starts to come together in small clumps. Tip
half this crumbly mixture into the tart tin and, using your
fingers, press it evenly up the sides of the tin. Press the
remainder onto the base. Chill the shortbread while you
preheat the oven to 170°C/330°F/Gas 3½.

Bake the shortbread on the middle shelf for about
25 minutes until golden brown. Remove from the oven
and, using a round-bladed knife, mark the base of the
shortbread into 6–8 fingers, cutting into but not through
the shortbread; this will make serving easier. Leave to
cool. Increase the oven temperature to 190°C/375°F/Gas 5.

Arrange the apricot halves cut side up in a single layer
in a roasting tray lined with baking parchment. Tuck the
lemon zest, vanilla pod and thyme amongst the apricots
and spoon over the lemon juice, honey and water. Bake
on the middle shelf for 20–25 minutes until tender and
starting to caramelize at the edges, spooning the pan
juices over the fruit halfway through. Leave to cool.

Tip the strained labneh into a bowl, add honey to taste
and the lemon zest, and mix to combine. Spoon into the
shortbread base, spread level and arrange the roasted
apricots on top. Drizzle over any pan juices and scatter
with blueberries and pistachios. Decorate with bee pollen
and flowers, if using, and serve immediately.

SWEET

112

PECAN, BOURBON & CHOCOLATE PIE

Pecan pie is an all-time classic and rightly so – what's not to love about the combination of crisp pastry shell filled with pecans baked in a sticky, rich, warming almost custardy sugariness…? I like to think that this pecan pie goes a little further, steps it up and shakes it up. The pie crust is coated in dark chocolate and the filling has a hit of smoky bourbon – neither ingredient overwhelming the toasty pecans, but rather enhancing them.

I had intended to make this pie with maple syrup in place of golden but I found it just a touch too sickly for my tastes. However, if you have this to hand and you prefer the taste then please feel free. Whichever syrup you use, this pie is begging for vanilla ice cream.

Brown sugar pastry
175g [1⅓ cups] plain [all-purpose] flour, plus extra for rolling out
a good pinch of salt
100g [½ cup minus 1 Tbsp] unsalted butter, diced and chilled
2 Tbsp maple sugar or soft light brown sugar
1 medium egg yolk
1 Tbsp ice-cold water
1 tsp cider vinegar or lemon juice

ingredients continued »

Start by making the brown sugar pastry. Tip the flour into a bowl and add the salt. Add the diced butter and cut the butter into the flour using either a round-bladed knife or palette knife. When the butter pieces are coated in butter and about half their original size, switch to using your hands to rub the butter in, working quickly and lightly. When there are only very small flecks of butter still visible, add the sugar and mix again to combine.

Make a well in the middle of the mixture, drop in the egg yolk, water and vinegar or lemon juice. Using the knife again, cut the wet ingredients into the dry then use your hands to continue mixing, but do not overwork the mixture. Turn the dough out onto the work surface, gather into a ball, flatten into a disc, cover with cling film [plastic wrap] and chill for at least 1 hour until firm.

Roll out the dough on a lightly floured surface to a thickness of 2–3mm [¹⁄₁₆–¹⁄₈in] and with a diameter of about 7.5cm [3in] wider than the tart tin. Carefully line the tin with the pastry, pressing it neatly into each groove and corner. Trim any excess from the top, prick the base with a fork and chill for 20–30 minutes while you preheat the oven to 180°C/350°F/Gas 4.

continued »

continued »

Filling
300g [3 cups] pecans
50g [1¾oz] dark [bittersweet] chocolate (70% cocoa solids), plus another 25g [1oz] to decorate
4 medium eggs
125g [scant ⅔ cup] soft dark brown sugar
125g [6 Tbsp] golden syrup
2 Tbsp bourbon
1 tsp vanilla extract or bean paste
50g [3½ Tbsp] unsalted butter, melted
1 tsp lemon juice or cider vinegar
a good pinch of sea salt flakes

You will need a 22-cm [8¾-in] tart tin with a removable base

Serves 8

Line the pastry case with foil and fill with baking rice, place on a baking sheet and bake on the middle shelf of the oven for about 20 minutes until golden. Remove the foil and rice and bake for a further 3–4 minutes to dry out the base. Remove from the oven and set aside while you prepare the filling.

Tip the pecans onto a baking sheet and toast in the oven for 3–4 minutes, then roughly chop. Reduce the oven temperature to 170°C/330°F/Gas 3½. Melt the chocolate either in a heatproof bowl in the microwave on a low setting or over a bowl of barely simmering water. Stir the chocolate until smooth, pour into the tart shell and spread to evenly cover the base.

Break the eggs into a bowl, add the sugar, golden syrup, bourbon and vanilla and whisk until smooth. Add the melted butter to the bowl along with the lemon juice and salt flakes. Add the chopped pecans and mix to combine.

Scoop the filling into the tart shell and spread evenly. Bake on the middle shelf of the oven for 30 minutes, after which time the filling should have the faintest wobble in the middle. Remove the tart from the oven and leave to cool at room temperature; the filling will continue to cook and set as it cools.

Once the tart is cool, melt the remaining chocolate and, using either a disposable piping [pastry] bag or teaspoon, drizzle the chocolate in a haphazard fashion over the top of tart. Ideally serve with a good scoop of vanilla ice cream.

RICOTTA & FIG TART

An Italian-inspired cheesecake tart. I implore you to use a good-quality
Italian ricotta and full-fat cream cheese for this tart – some cheaper
brands of ricotta taste of very little and bring almost nothing to a dish.
I also like to use black-skinned figs with deep red centres for contrast.

Crostata pastry
175g [1⅓ cups] plain [all-purpose]
  flour, plus extra for rolling out
40g [⅓ cup] fine semolina or
  rice flour
a pinch of salt
125g [½ cup plus 1 Tbsp] unsalted
  butter, chilled and diced
50g [¼ cup] caster [granulated]
  sugar
1 tsp finely grated lemon zest,
  plus 2 tsp juice
1 medium egg yolk
1–1½ Tbsp ice-cold water

Filling
300g [1⅓ cups] ricotta
225g [1 cup] cream cheese
75g [6 Tbsp] caster [granulated]
  sugar
2 Tbsp clear honey
3 medium eggs, lightly beaten
100ml [⅓ cup plus 1 Tbsp] double
  [heavy] cream
1 tsp finely grated lemon zest
1 tsp vanilla bean paste
1 Tbsp cornflour [cornstarch]
a pinch of salt
4–5 ripe figs, thinly sliced

You will need a 21–22-cm
  [8–8¾-in] tart tin,
  4cm [1½in] deep

Serves 8

Start by making the crostata pastry. Tip the flour into a
large bowl, add the semolina or rice flour and salt and mix
to combine. Add the diced butter and cut into the flour
using a round-bladed knife until the butter pieces are
half their original size. Continue rubbing in using your
fingertips until there are only small flecks of butter still
visible. Add the sugar and lemon zest and mix to combine.

Make a well in the middle of the mixture, add the egg yolk,
lemon juice and 1 tablespoon cold water. Mix using the
round-bladed or palette knife to bring the dough together
in clumps, adding a drop more water if it is dry. Bring
the pastry together in your hands, being careful not to
overwork it, shape into a ball, flatten into a disc, wrap
in cling film [plastic wrap] and chill for at least 2 hours.

Dust the work surface with flour and roll out the dough
into a neat round that is 2–3mm [¹⁄₁₆–¹⁄₈in] thick and 8cm
[3¼in] wider in diameter than the tart tin. Line the tin
with the pastry, pressing it neatly into the corners. Trim
any excess off the top, prick the base with a fork and chill
for 30 minutes. Preheat the oven to 180°C/350°F/Gas 4.

Line the pastry shell with foil and baking rice and place
the tin on a solid baking sheet. Bake in the middle of the
oven for 20 minutes until the top edge is starting to turn
golden. Remove the foil and rice and bake for 3–4 minutes
to dry out the base of the tart shell. Leave to cool slightly.

Tip the ricotta into a bowl, add the cream cheese, sugar
and honey and beat until smooth. Add the eggs, cream,
lemon zest, vanilla, cornflour and salt and whisk again
until smooth. Pour the mixture into the tart shell, slide the
tart into the oven and bake for 20 minutes until the top
is barely set. Arrange the figs over the filling and bake for
a further 20 minutes, by which time the figs will be juicy
and the filling set and starting to turn golden at the edges.
Serve either at room temperature or lightly chilled.

MINCEMEAT CROSTATA

This tart wouldn't look out of place at your next festive gathering, with its plump, spiced dried fruit, fancy pastry plaits and dusting of snowy icing sugar. It's a wonderful alternative to Christmas pudding. Serve it warm with brandy butter, softly whipped cream or some top-notch ice cream – vanilla or stem ginger would be my preference.

Decorative pastry work and lattice can look daunting but it's a matter of concentration. Brew a mug of tea and settle in for a half-hour of creativity.

Mincemeat

1 large Bramley apple
100g [¾ cup] raisins
75g [½ cup] sultanas [golden raisins]
75g [½ cup] currants
50g [scant ½ cup] dried cranberries
30g [¼ cup] chopped candied peel
100g [½ cup] soft dark brown sugar
100g [¾ cup] almonds, roughly chopped
finely grated zest and juice of ½ lemon
finely grated zest and juice of ½ orange
4 Tbsp Calvados or brandy
1 tsp ground cinnamon
¼ tsp ground allspice
a good grating of nutmeg
a good pinch of sea salt flakes
75g [⅓ cup] unsalted butter, diced
150g [5¼oz] marzipan

Crostata pastry

250g [1 cup plus 2 Tbsp] plain [all-purpose] flour, plus extra for rolling out
50g [¼ cup] fine semolina
a pinch of salt
175g [¾ cup plus 1 tsp] unsalted butter, chilled and diced
75g [6 Tbsp] caster [granulated] sugar, plus extra for sprinkling
finely grated zest of ½ lemon, plus 1 teaspoon juice
1 medium egg, plus 1 medium egg yolk
1–2 Tbsp ice-cold water
2 Tbsp milk
icing [confectioners'] sugar, for dusting

You will need a 23-cm [9-in] fluted tart tin with a removable base

Serves 10

Start by making the mincemeat – which can, and should, be prepared a day or so in advance of baking your crostata. Preheat the oven to 170°C/330°F/Gas 3½. Peel and coarsely grate the apple into a large mixing bowl. Add all the remaining ingredients apart from the butter and marzipan and mix well to combine. Line a roasting tray with a double thickness of baking parchment and spoon the mincemeat into the lined tray, cover tightly with foil and cook on the middle shelf for 30 minutes, stirring twice, until the fruit is plump and juicy. Add the butter, mix to combine and return to the oven, loosely covered, for another 5 minutes. Stir again, spoon into a clean bowl or plastic food box and leave to cool and absorb any remaining liquid. Cover and leave in a cool part of the kitchen until ready to bake.

To make the crostata pastry, tip the flour, semolina and salt into a large mixing bowl. Add the chilled diced butter and rub into the dry ingredients using your fingertips (or a food processor if you don't mind the extra washing up). Add 75g [6 Tbsp] of the sugar and the lemon zest and mix to combine. Make a well in the middle of the mixture and add the whole egg, extra yolk, ice-cold water and lemon juice. Use a round-bladed or palette knife to bring the dough together – it will be quite sticky – gather into a ball, flatten into a disc, cover with cling film [plastic wrap] and chill for at least 2 hours or until firm.

Lightly dust the work surface with flour and divide the dough in half. Cover one portion with cling film and keep it chilled for the time being. Roll the other portion into a neat round, 3cm [1¼in] larger all round than the tart tin. Carefully line the tin, leaving any excess pastry hanging over the sides, and chill for 20 minutes while you preheat the oven to 180°C/350°F/Gas 4, placing a solid baking sheet on the middle shelf to heat up.

Trim any excess pastry from the top of the tin, prick the base with a fork, line the tart shell with foil, fill with baking rice and blind bake for 20 minutes until the crust is pale golden. Remove the foil and rice and cook for a further 2 minutes.

SWEET

continued »

continued »

To make the lattice top, dust the work surface with flour and roll out the remaining pastry into a round, about 4cm [1½in] larger than the top of the tart tin. Using a pastry wheel (or long knife) and ruler as a guide, cut the dough into narrow strips each 3–4mm [⅛in] wide. Take 3 dough strips of similar length, pinch them together at the top and neatly plait into a long strand, trying not to stretch the dough as you plait. Place on a parchment-lined baking sheet and repeat with the remaining dough. Any off-cuts can be re-rolled and stamped into little stars. Chill for 10 minutes.

Dust the work surface with icing sugar and roll the marzipan into a neat 20-cm [8-in] round. Spoon half of the mincemeat into the tart shell in an even layer, place the marzipan disc on top and spoon over the remaining mincemeat. Brush the edge of the tart with a little water or milk. Carefully arrange the plaited strips across the tart over the mincemeat, press the edges together to seal and cut off any excess pastry. Arrange the stars around the edge, brush the plaits and stars with milk and sprinkle with sugar.

Slide the pie onto the hot baking sheet and bake for 40–45 minutes until the pastry is crisp and golden.

Leave to cool slightly then serve the warm crostata dusted with icing sugar and with brandy butter, softly whipped cream or some marvellous ice cream alongside.

BANANA & MISO
CARAMEL GALETTE

I had it in my mind to make a banoffee pie-type tart for months, but for the life of me I couldn't make it work the way I wanted and hoped. And then this happened. Miso has a wonderful umami taste which works brilliantly in caramel, and caramel works well with bananas, and chocolate and peanuts…

And whatever happens you must serve this galette with extra caramel sauce and vanilla ice cream, or lightly whipped double cream.

Cream cheese pastry
150g [1 cup plus 2 Tbsp] plain [all-purpose] flour, plus extra for rolling out
½ tsp baking powder
25g [2 Tbsp] caster [granulated] sugar
a pinch of salt
75g [⅓ cup] unsalted butter, chilled and diced
75g [⅓ cup] cream cheese, chilled
50g [½ cup] ground almonds
1 medium egg yolk
1 Tbsp cold milk

Miso caramel sauce
125g [⅔ cup] caster [granulated] sugar
1 Tbsp hot water
150ml [⅔ cup] double [heavy] cream
75g [6 Tbsp] light muscovado sugar
50g [3½ Tbsp] unsalted butter
2 Tbsp white miso paste
1 tsp vanilla bean paste
a pinch of sea salt flakes

ingredients continued »

Prepare the cream cheese pastry following the instructions on page 13 and chill for at least 2 hours.

Meanwhile, make the miso caramel sauce. Tip the caster sugar into a medium-sized, solid-bottomed saucepan and add the hot water. Set the pan over a low heat to dissolve the sugar without stirring, but swirling the pan to dissolve the sugar evenly. Bring the syrup to the boil and carefully brush the inside of the pan with water to dissolve any crystals that may have formed and are clinging to the sides of the pan. Cook steadily until the syrup becomes a rich amber caramel – you will most likely need to swirl the pan to ensure that the caramel cooks evenly. Carefully slide the pan off the heat and add the cream, muscovado, butter, miso, vanilla and sea salt. The caramel may hiss and bubble furiously, so take care.

Return the pan to a low heat to re-melt any hardened caramel, simmer for 30 seconds to combine all of the ingredients, remove from the heat and leave to cool.

Preheat the oven to 190°C/375°F/Gas 5 and place a solid baking sheet on the middle shelf to heat up at the same time.

To make the filling, peel the bananas and cut in half from top to bottom. Melt the butter and sugar in a large frying pan over a medium–high heat. Add half of the banana halves, cut side down, and cook quickly to lightly caramelize in the butter. Carefully remove from the pan and set aside while you caramelize the remaining bananas in the same pan.

continued »

Filling

6–8 bananas, depending on size

40g [3 Tbsp] unsalted butter

1 Tbsp caster [granulated] sugar,
    plus a little extra for sprinkling

50g [1¾oz] dark [bittersweet]
    chocolate, finely chopped
    (or chips)

50g [⅓ cup] salted peanuts,
    roughly chopped

1 Tbsp milk, to glaze

Serves 6

Dust the work surface with flour and roll the pastry out into a neat round with a diameter of 32–33cm [12½–13in], and slide the pastry onto a parchment-lined baking sheet. Spread 1–2 tablespoons of the miso caramel into the middle of the pastry, leaving a 5-cm [2-in] border all around. Scatter over the chopped chocolate and half of the peanuts. Arrange the bananas on top, cut side uppermost, packing them tightly together.

Fold the edges of the pastry over to create a border, leaving the middle of the tart exposed. Brush the pastry edges with milk and sprinkle with sugar, drizzle the bananas with a little more caramel and scatter over the remaining peanuts.

Slide the galette onto the hot baking sheet in the oven and cook for 20 minutes. Reduce the heat to 180°C/350°F/Gas 4 and cook for a further 10 minutes until the pastry is golden and crisp and the bananas are caramelized.

Cool for a few minutes and then serve the galette with the remaining warmed caramel, and some vanilla ice cream.

SWEET

PLUM & ALMOND TART

This is one of the very first recipes that I tested for this book. Although very happy with the results, I decided to fiddle with the method and quantities over and over until I ended up right back where I started. It's a classic tart and for very good reason – if it ain't broke, don't fix it.

I have used plums – and in this instance slightly firmer than ripe fruit – but I urge you to try greengages or apricots when in season.

Sweet pastry

250g [1 cup plus 2 Tbsp] plain [all-purpose] flour, plus extra for rolling out

a pinch of salt

150g [⅔ cup] unsalted butter, chilled and diced

75g [½ cup] icing [confectioners'] sugar

2 medium egg yolks (reserve 1 egg white for brushing the base)

2 Tbsp ice-cold water

2 tsp lemon juice

Filling

175g [¾ cup plus 1 tsp] unsalted butter, at room temperature

175g [¾ cup plus 2 Tbsp] caster [granulated] sugar, plus 2 tsp for the top

1 tsp vanilla bean paste

3 medium eggs, lightly beaten

finely grated zest of ½ lemon

175g [1¾ cups] ground almonds

25g [3 Tbsp] plain [all-purpose] flour

a pinch of salt

700g [1lb 9oz] plums, halved, stoned and thinly sliced

40g [½ cup] flaked [slivered] almonds

1 Tbsp golden caster or granulated sugar

You will need a 28-cm [11-in] loose-bottomed tart tin

Serves 10

Prepare the sweet pastry using the ingredients on this page and following the instructions on page 11. Chill for at least 2 hours.

Dust the work surface with flour and roll out the pastry into a round about 3mm [⅛in] thick and use to line the tart tin. Press the dough neatly and evenly into the corners and grooves of the tin and trim off the excess from the top. Prick the base with a fork and chill for 30 minutes while you preheat the oven to 180°C/350°F/Gas 4.

Line the pastry shell with foil, fill with baking rice, place on a solid baking sheet and blind bake for 20 minutes until pale golden. Remove the foil and rice and bake for a further 4–5 minutes to dry out the bottom of the tart shell. Lightly beat the reserved egg white and brush over the base of the tart. Return to the oven for a further minute.

Meanwhile, make the filling. Cream together the softened butter, sugar and vanilla until pale and light (this is easiest in a free-standing mixer but not impossible by hand). Gradually add the beaten eggs, mixing well between each addition. Add the lemon zest and mix again before adding the ground almonds, flour and salt. Beat until smooth, cover and set aside at room temperature until needed.

Leave the tart shell to cool before filling. Spread the filling evenly into the tart shell and arrange the plums on top, slightly fanning the slices over the filling. Sprinkle the flaked almonds and the 2 teaspoons caster sugar on top. Bake on the middle shelf of the oven for about 55 minutes, turning halfway through. The filling will be risen and golden brown, the pastry crisp and the plums starting to caramelize. Leave to cool to just warm and serve with crème fraîche or double cream.

PANDOWDY SWAMP PIE

Pandowdy is a fruit pie, cooked in a skillet, with a cobbler-like topping. The swamp element comes from flooding the cooked pie with cream and returning it to the oven where the cream and fruit juices combine into a delicious fruity soup.

Cream cheese pastry

225g [1¾ cups] plain [all-purpose] flour, plus extra for rolling out

1 tsp baking powder

40g [3¼ Tbsp] caster [granulated] sugar

a pinch of salt

115g [½ cup] unsalted butter, chilled and diced

115g [½ cup] cream cheese, chilled

75g [¾ cup] ground almonds

2 medium egg yolks

1½ Tbsp cold milk or water

Filling

5 peaches, quartered, stoned and sliced

200g [7oz] raspberries

200g [7oz] blueberries

3 Tbsp caster [granulated] sugar, plus extra for sprinkling

juice of ½ lemon

1½ Tbsp cornflour [cornstarch]

1 tsp vanilla bean paste

1 medium egg, separated

1 Tbsp demerara [turbinado] sugar

175ml [¾ cup] double [heavy] cream

You will need a cast-iron skillet or ovenproof frying pan with a base measurement of 20cm [8in] and top of 25cm [10in], and a 5-cm [2-in] plain round cutter

Serves 6–8

Prepare the cream cheese pastry using the ingredients on this page and following the instructions on page 13. Chill for at least 2 hours until firm.

Divide the pastry in half, with one portion slightly larger than the other. Dust the work surface with flour and roll the larger pastry portion out to a round about 3mm [1/8in] thick and large enough to cover the base and sides of the skillet, with a little extra pastry hanging over the sides. Line the tin and refrigerate with the remaining pastry while you prepare the filling and preheat the oven to 190°C/375°F/Gas 5.

To make the filling, mix the fruit, caster sugar, lemon juice, cornflour and vanilla together well. Scoop the filling and any residual juices into the pastry-lined skillet.

Roll the remaining pastry out to a thickness of 3mm [1/8in] and, using the cutter, stamp out rounds. Gather the scraps together into a ball and re-roll and stamp out more rounds. Completely cover the top of the pie with pastry rounds in a patchwork, haphazard fashion, leaving the odd gap for steam to escape. Cut off any excess pastry from the side of the skillet and crimp the edges to seal. Beat the egg white until foamy, brush over the pie and sprinkle the demerara sugar over the top. Bake on a baking sheet on the middle shelf for 20 minutes. Turn the pie around, reduce the temperature to 180°C/350°F/Gas 4 and bake for a further 20–25 minutes until the pastry is crisp, golden and the fruit filling is tender and bubbling.

Meanwhile, whisk together the cream and egg yolk. Cut a few holes in the top of the pastry to create a few gaps and carefully pour the cream mixture into the pie through the holes. Don't worry if some floods over the top – this is the swampy part of the pie. Bake for a further 10 minutes to set the cream and then serve the pie hot.

MALTED CHOCOLATE SILK

I first made a version of this tart many moons ago when catering for events. This updated version – with toasted rye flakes, muscovado sugar and barley malt – is much improved.

When it comes to decorating this tart, keep 2 tablespoons of filling back: fold one into some whipped cream to make chocolate kisses, and pipe the remainder into even smaller kisses between the gaps.

continued »

Pecan & rye crust

200g [2 cups] pecans

75g [2¾oz] rye flakes

100g [½ cup] light muscovado
  sugar

½ tsp ground cinnamon

a pinch of sea salt flakes

75g [⅓ cup] unsalted butter,
  melted

Filling

350g [12¼oz] dark [bittersweet]
  chocolate (70% cocoa solids),
  chopped

100g [½ cup minus 1 Tbsp]
  unsalted butter, diced

75g [6 Tbsp] light muscovado
  sugar

4 Tbsp barley malt extract

3 medium eggs

1 tsp vanilla bean paste

½ tsp sea salt flakes

150ml [⅔ cup] double [heavy]
  cream

To serve

300ml [1¼ cups] double [heavy]
  cream

1 Tbsp barley malt extract

You will need a 20-cm [8-in]
  tart ring and a piping [pastry]
  bag fitted with an open star
  nozzle [tip]

Serves 10–12

Preheat the oven to 180°C/350°F/Gas 4.

Spread the pecans out in a roasting tray and the
rye flakes onto another and toast both in the oven for
4 minutes. Leave to cool and then whizz the pecans in a
food processor until finely chopped but still with some
crunch and texture. Tip the nuts and rye flakes into a
bowl, add the sugar, cinnamon and sea salt. Add the
melted butter and mix to combine.

Set the tart ring on a baking sheet lined with baking
parchment. Tip the nut mixture into the tart ring, press
the crust to evenly cover the base and sides and bake for
5 minutes until crisp. Leave to cool.

To make the filling, melt the chocolate and butter together
in a heatproof bowl over a pan of simmering water, but
do not allow the bottom of the bowl to touch the water.
Stir until smooth then remove from the heat. Whisk the
sugar, malt extract, eggs, vanilla and sea salt in another
heatproof bowl, set this over the simmering water and
whisk constantly for about 5 minutes until the mixture is
hot to the touch and thickens slightly – if you have a sugar
thermometer, pop it into the bowl and it should reach
62–63°C/143–145°F when the eggs are cooked. Remove
from the heat and leave to cool for a couple of minutes.

Stirring gently and constantly, pour the melted chocolate
into the bowl until just combined. Add the cream and mix
again until silky. Pour the mixture into the tart shell, cool
to room temperature, cover and chill overnight until set.

Twenty minutes before you are ready to serve, remove the
tart from the fridge. Remove the tart ring – this is easiest
by very quickly flashing a blowtorch around the outside
of the ring. Whip the cream until it will just hold a peak
and spoon half of it into a disposable piping bag, snip the
end into a point and pipe cream in neat kisses on top of
the tart. Fold the barley extract into the remaining cream,
spoon into the piping bag fitted with the star nozzle and
pipe rosettes among the kisses. Use a warmed knife to
cut the chocolate silk into neat slices and serve with any
remaining cream on the side.

SWEET

SUMMER FRUIT & HAZELNUT MOUSSELINE TART

This tart provides you with a great opportunity to make use of the sweetest, juiciest and most beautiful summer fruit you can find. Strawberries, raspberries, cherries, figs and peaches are all wonderful together, but a handful of red or white currants, wild strawberries, blackberries and sliced ripe plums would all be welcome additions or substitutions.

250g [8¾oz] strawberries, hulled and halved

200g [7oz] cherries, stoned and halved

4 ripe figs, quartered or sliced

2 peaches, stoned and sliced

200g [7oz] raspberries

icing [confectioners'] sugar, for dusting (optional)

Sweet pastry

200g [1½ cups] plain [all-purpose] flour, plus extra for rolling out

a good pinch of salt

125g [½ cup plus 1 Tbsp] unsalted butter, diced and chilled

40g [4½ Tbsp] icing [confectioners'] sugar

1 medium egg yolk

1–2 Tbsp ice-cold water

2 tsp lemon juice

Hazelnut mousseline

150g [¾ cup] caster [granulated] sugar

1 Tbsp hot water

100g [¾ cup] blanched hazelnuts

300ml [1¼ cups] whole milk

4 medium egg yolks

1 Tbsp cornflour [cornstarch]

1 tsp vanilla bean paste

200ml [generous ¾ cup] double [heavy] cream

You will need a 25-cm [10-in] tart tin

Serves 8–10

Prepare the sweet pastry following the instructions on page 11 and chill for at least 2 hours.

Make the hazelnut mousseline while the pastry is chilling. Tip 100g [½ cup] of the sugar into a non-stick frying pan, add the hot water and set the pan over a low–medium heat to gently dissolve the sugar without stirring. Increase the heat, bring the syrup to the boil and continue to cook until the sugar becomes a deep amber caramel. Working quickly, tip the hazelnuts into the pan and, using a lightly oiled fork, stir to coat the nuts in the caramel. When the hazelnuts are lightly toasted and enrobed in caramel, tip the contents of the pan onto a sheet of baking parchment. Leave to cool and harden.

Pour the milk into a smallish saucepan and heat to just below boiling point. In a bowl, whisk the egg yolks with the remaining 50g [¼ cup] sugar, the cornflour and vanilla. Pour the hot milk into the bowl and whisk constantly until thoroughly combined. Return the mixture to the saucepan and set the pan over a low–medium heat. Slowly bring to the boil, whisking constantly to cook the eggs and cornflour and to thicken the custard. Once boiling, allow the custard to gently bubble and blip for 30 seconds to cook out the cornflour; taste it and if you can still detect the chalkiness from the cornflour, cook for another 10 seconds or so. Strain into a clean bowl, cover the surface of the custard with cling film [plastic wrap] and leave to cool. Once completely cold, chill until ready to use.

continued »

continued »

Dust the work surface with flour and roll
out the pastry into a neat round 2–3mm
[^{1}/$_{16}$–^{1}/$_8$in] thick, and with a diameter a
generous 6cm [2½in] wider than the base
of the tart tin. Carefully line the tart tin
with the pastry, trim the excess from the
top and prick the base of the tart shell
with a fork. Chill for 20 minutes while you
preheat the oven to 180°C/350°F/Gas 4.

Line the tart shell with foil and baking rice
and place on a solid baking sheet. Cook
on the middle shelf of the oven for about
15 minutes until the top edge of the pastry
starts to turn golden. Remove the foil and
rice and cook for a further 4 minutes or so
until the pastry is crisp and golden all over.
Leave to cool before filling.

Break the caramelized hazelnuts into
pieces and whizz in a food processor
until finely ground. Continue whizzing
for a further minute or two until the
praline starts to turn into a nearly smooth,
nutty paste.

Whip the cream until it will hold a peak
then fold in the chilled custard followed
by the hazelnut caramel paste. Spoon
this hazelnut mousseline into the tart shell
and spread level. Arrange all the fruit
on top of the hazelnut mousseline – as
neatly or haphazardly as you like. Finally,
dust with icing sugar if the mood takes
you, and serve.

LEMON & PINE NUT TART

This is my take on the Italian classic *Torta della Nonna*, which has a light custardy filling and either a pastry top and bottom or, as I have made it here, with a pastry bottom and topping of pine nuts.

Pastry

100g [½ cup minus 1 Tbsp] unsalted butter, softened
50g [¼ cup] caster [granulated] sugar
2 medium egg yolks
200g [1½ cups] plain [all-purpose] flour, plus extra for rolling out
¼ tsp baking powder
a pinch of salt
1–2 Tbsp cold milk or water

Filling

400ml [1²/₃ cups] whole milk
100ml [¹/₃ cup plus 1 Tbsp] double [heavy] cream
6 medium egg yolks
125g [²/₃ cup] caster [granulated] sugar
3 level Tbsp cornflour [cornstarch]
finely grated zest and juice of 2 lemons
a pinch of salt
75g [generous ½ cup] pine nuts
1–2 Tbsp icing [confectioners'] sugar

You will need a 20-cm [8-in] loose-bottomed tart tin, 3.5cm [1¼in] deep

Serves 8

To make the pastry, cream the softened butter and sugar until pale and light. Add the egg yolks and mix until thoroughly combined. Sift the flour, baking powder and salt into the bowl and mix until incorporated and the pastry dough is smooth, adding enough cold milk or water to bring the dough together. Flatten the dough into a disc, wrap in cling film [plastic wrap] and chill for at least 1 hour.

Meanwhile, prepare the filling. Heat the milk and cream in a medium saucepan until just below boiling point. In a bowl, whisk the egg yolks with the sugar, cornflour, lemon zest and juice, and salt. Pour the hot milk into the bowl, whisking constantly. Return the mixture to the pan and cook over a low–medium heat, whisking constantly until thickened and the cornflour has been cooked out. Pour into a clean bowl, cover the surface with cling film to prevent a skin forming and cool to room temperature.

Lightly dust the work surface with flour, roll out the pastry to a thickness of about 3mm [¹/₈in] and line the tart tin. The pastry is a little crumbly so simply patch any holes or cracks. Trim off any excess pastry from the top of the tin, prick the base with a fork and chill for 30 minutes while you preheat the oven to 180°C/350°F/Gas 4, placing a solid baking sheet on the middle shelf of the oven to heat up.

Spoon the cold lemony filling into the pastry case and spread level with the back of a spoon. Scatter the top of the tart with the pine nuts and bake on the hot baking sheet for about 30 minutes until the pastry is golden and the filling set.

Leave to cool, then dust with icing sugar to serve.

QUINCE GALETTE DES ROIS

Pastry shops all over France traditionally sell this *galette des rois* for Epiphany (Twelfth Night) on 6 January, to celebrate the arrival of The Three Kings in Bethlehem to visit baby Jesus. It often has a ceramic charm or *fève* (bean) baked into the almond filling and the lucky person receiving the charm in their portion becomes king or queen for the day.

The traditional version is filled with an almond cream, or frangipane, to which I have added either sliced poached quince or quince paste if fresh are unavailable. You could also add a handful of chopped dark chocolate or candied peel as an alternative or addition to the quince.

Puff pastry
250g [1 cup plus 2 Tbsp] unsalted butter, chilled
150g [1 cup plus 2 Tbsp] plain [all-purpose] flour, plus extra
100g [¾ cup minus ½ Tbsp] strong white flour
a pinch of salt
1 medium egg yolk, plus 1 beaten egg for glazing
100–125ml [6–8 Tbsp] ice-cold water
1 tsp lemon juice

Poached quince
600ml [2½ cups] water
200g [1 cup] caster sugar
juice of 1 lemon
1 vanilla pod [bean], split in half lengthways
2 star anise
1 bay leaf
2 quince (or 2–3 Tbsp quince paste/jam)

Frangipane
100g [½ cup minus 1 Tbsp] unsalted butter, at room temperature
100g [½ cup] caster sugar
2 medium eggs, lightly beaten
125g [1¼ cups] ground almonds
1 Tbsp plain [all-purpose] flour
2 Tbsp brandy
1 tsp finely grated lemon zest
a good pinch of sea salt flakes

Serves 12

Prepare the puff pastry, ideally the day before, following the instructions on page 12 until the final roll and fold, then chill for at least 2 hours.

To poach the quince, pour the water into a medium-sized saucepan, add the sugar, lemon juice, halved vanilla pod, star anise and bay leaf. Peel the quince, cut into quarters and drop into the pan – do not worry about removing the cores at this stage. The fruit should fit snugly in the pan and just be covered by the syrup – top up with a little more water if necessary. Place the pan over a medium heat and bring slowly to the boil to dissolve the sugar. Cover the fruit with a circle of baking parchment and simmer gently for about 25 minutes until tender when tested with the point of a knife. Remove from the heat and leave to cool in the syrup.

To make the frangipane, cream together the softened butter and sugar until pale and light. Add the beaten eggs and mix again. Add the remaining ingredients and mix until well combined. Cover and chill for 30 minutes.

Drain the quince from the poaching liquid, pat dry and carefully remove the cores and seeds. Thinly slice the quince – if they are large you may not need all of them for the filling, but you can serve any extra alongside.

Dust the work surface with flour and divide the pastry into 2 pieces, one slightly larger than the other. Roll the smaller piece out into a neat round, about 2mm [¹⁄₁₆in] thick. Using a plate or tart or cake tin as a guide, cut out a

continued »

22-cm [8¾-in] round from the pastry and slide onto a parchment-lined baking sheet. Arrange the sliced quince in a single layer in the middle of the pastry round, leaving a 2-cm [¾-in] border all around the outside (or spread the quince paste, if using, into the middle of the pastry).

Spoon or pipe the frangipane on top and, using a palette knife, spread into an even layer, covering the quince and with neat straight-edged sides. Chill for 30 minutes.

Roll the second piece of pastry out into a round of similar thickness as the first, cut into a 30-cm [12-in] round and carefully roll the pastry disc around the rolling pin. Brush the exposed pastry edges of the frangipane-topped pastry with beaten egg and unroll the larger pastry round over the top to evenly cover the frangipane. Use your hands to smooth the pastry over the frangipane to neatly cover the top and sides. Press the bottom edge to seal and trim off any excess pastry.

Brush with beaten egg and chill for 30 minutes while you preheat the oven to 180°C/350°F/Gas 4, placing a solid baking sheet on the middle shelf to heat up at the same time.

Using a small, sharp knife, 'knock up' the cut sides of the pastry – hold the knife blade horizontally to the cut edges and make small tapping cuts all around the galette – this helps the pastry layers to separate into delicate flakes. Using the point of the knife, score a decorative pattern into the top of the galette, cutting into but not through the pastry.

Bake the galette on the hot baking sheet for 40–45 minutes until golden brown and crisp – you may need to turn the tray around in the oven halfway through baking.

Leave to cool and cut into slices to serve.

SWEET

135

SALTED TA-HONEY PIE

This recipe is inspired by the now famous Salty Honey Pie served at Four and Twenty Blackbirds in New York City. I have added tahini and chocolate to my pie as they are natural bedfellows and seem to bring out the best in each other. Add a pinch of sea salt flakes and a touch of vinegar to round things off and this is what you get.

Tahini pastry

100g [½ cup minus 1 Tbsp] unsalted butter, at room temperature

50g [scant ¼ cup] tahini

50g [5¾ Tbsp] icing [confectioners'] sugar

a good pinch of salt

2 medium egg yolks

200g/1½ cups plain [all-purpose] flour, plus extra for rolling out

1 tsp ground cinnamon

1 Tbsp ice-cold water

50g [1¾oz] dark [bittersweet] chocolate (70% cocoa solids), chopped

Filling

175g [¾ cup] unsalted butter

225g [¾ cup] clear honey

125g [²/₃ cup] soft light brown sugar

3 medium eggs, plus 2 medium yolks

125ml [½ cup] double [heavy] cream

2 rounded Tbsp tahini

2 tsp cider vinegar

2 tsp vanilla bean paste

a large pinch of sea salt flakes

1 tsp each, black and white sesame seeds

You will need a 20-cm [8-in] fluted tart tin

Serves 8

Start by making the tahini pastry. Combine the butter, tahini, icing sugar and salt in a bowl and beat until soft and light. Add the egg yolks and mix again to combine. Fold in the flour, cinnamon and water and beat until combined, but do not overwork the pastry. Add a little more water if needed to bring the dough together. Flatten the dough into a disc, wrap in cling film [plastic wrap] and chill for at least 2 hours or overnight.

Roll out the pastry on a lightly floured surface into a neat round that is 3–4cm [1¼–1½in] wider all round than the tart tin. Carefully line the tin with the pastry, pressing it into the ridges and corners. Trim off the excess from the top, crimp the edges and chill for 30 minutes while you preheat the oven to 180°C/350°F/Gas 4.

Prick the base of the tart shell with a fork, line with foil, fill with baking rice and cook on a solid baking sheet for 15 minutes. Remove the foil and rice and bake for a further 2 minutes to crisp the base. Meanwhile, melt the chocolate in a heatproof bowl either over a pan of barely simmering water or in a microwave on a low setting. Stir until smooth and then spoon into the baked tart shell. Spread to evenly cover the base and set aside.

To make the filling, gently melt the butter in a small pan and continue to cook until the milk solids start to turn golden brown and the butter smells nutty and toasted. Scoop into a bowl and cool slightly. Add the honey, sugar, eggs and extra yolks, cream, tahini, vinegar, vanilla and salt flakes. Whisk to combine. Carefully pour into the tart shell, sprinkle the sesame seeds over the top, slide the tart back into the oven and cook for 40–45 minutes until the filling has puffed up at the edges and is golden brown and set, with a slight wobble. Serve at room temperature.

SAVOURY

VEAL & PORK SAUSAGE ROLLS
WITH SAGE & FENNEL SEEDS

A classy take on the humble sausage roll using a mixture of veal and pork and Italian-inspired seasoning. I like to shape these sausage rolls into bite-size morsels – making them perfect party nibbles. They can be prepared in advance and cooked just before serving. Feel free to make them larger as you see fit or your appetite dictates.

350g [¾lb] all-butter puff pastry (see page 12 for homemade)

Filling
250g [8¾oz] minced [ground] veal
250g [8¾oz] good-quality sausage meat
4 spring onions [scallions], finely sliced
1 fat garlic clove, very finely chopped
1 Tbsp finely chopped sage
2 Tbsp fresh breadcrumbs
2 Tbsp freshly grated Parmesan
1 tsp fennel seeds, lightly crushed
a good pinch of dried chilli flakes [red pepper flakes]
2 Tbsp milk
1 egg, for glazing
salt and freshly ground black pepper

Makes 20

Prepare the filling. Tip the veal and sausage meat into a mixing bowl. Add the spring onions, garlic and chopped sage. Add the breadcrumbs and Parmesan, fennel seeds and chilli flakes. Season well with salt and black pepper and mix well to combine – you'll find this easier to do with your hands.

Roll out the puff pastry on a lightly floured surface into a neat square, about 2mm [¹/₁₆in] thick. Trim the right hand edge to neaten. Divide the sausage mixture into three and, using damp hands, shape one piece into a long, thin sausage, roughly the same thickness as a chipolata – no thicker – and the same length as the pastry. Place on the right hand side of the pastry and brush the pastry on the other side of the filling with milk. Roll the sausage over in the pastry to encase and seal. Cut into one long sausage roll. Repeat with another third of the filling and pastry, and then the same again with the remaining third.

Cut the long rolls into 6–8-cm [2½–3¼-in] lengths and arrange on a baking sheet lined with baking parchment. Beat the egg with any remaining milk and brush over the top of each sausage roll. Chill the rolls for 30 minutes while you preheat the oven to 200°C/400°F/Gas 6.

Brush the rolls again with more egg wash, cut 3 small slashes into the top of each and bake on the middle shelf of the oven for 25 minutes until the filling is cooked through and the pastry crisp and golden.

BEEF & CHORIZO EMPANADAS WITH CHIMICHURRI

Empanadas are (more often than not) savoury hand pies that are found all over South America with a variety of fillings – beef, chicken, prawns, squash, beans… I've gone for the more Argentine option and filled mine with beef pepped up with some chorizo. Served with a chimichurri sauce, they are a delicious snack but one that is most likely far from the norm in Buenos Aires and thereabouts.

Filling

2 Tbsp olive oil
1 onion, finely chopped
2 garlic cloves, finely chopped
½ tsp ground cumin
½ tsp cayenne or smoked paprika
½ tsp dried oregano
400g [14oz] minced [ground] beef
85g [3oz] chorizo, finely diced
1 Tbsp tomato purée [paste]
85g [3oz] roasted red [bell] pepper
  or Peppadews, drained and
  chopped
75g [½ cup] raisins
100ml [⅓ cup] beef stock
½ tsp caster [granulated] sugar
75g [¾ cup] stoned black olives
salt and freshly ground
  black pepper

Pastry

350g [2⅔ cups] plain [all-purpose]
  flour, plus extra for rolling out
½ tsp smoked paprika
175g [¾ cup plus 1 tsp] unsalted
  butter
7 Tbsp milk
1 tsp cider (or white wine) vinegar
1 medium egg, beaten, for glazing

Chimichurri

2 garlic cloves, crushed
1 shallot, finely chopped
½ red chilli, deseeded and
  finely chopped
2 Tbsp chopped flat-leaf parsley
2 Tbsp chopped coriander
  [cilantro]
1 Tbsp roughly chopped oregano
2 Tbsp red wine vinegar
a good pinch of sea salt flakes
150ml [⅔ cup] extra virgin
  olive oil
a squeeze of lemon juice

You will need a 14-cm [5½-in]
  plain round cutter or saucer

Makes 12

To make the filling, heat the olive oil in a pan, add the onion and cook over a low–medium heat until soft but not coloured. Add the garlic and cook for a further minute. Add the spices and dried oregano and cook for another 30 seconds until aromatic, then add the beef and chorizo and cook over a high heat until browned. Add the tomato paste, cook for 1 minute then add the red pepper or Peppadews, raisins and stock. Add the sugar, season well, stir to combine, cover and cook over a low–medium heat for about 30 minutes until almost all of the liquid has been cooked off. Remove from the heat, check the seasoning and leave to cool.

To make the pastry, sift the flour into a bowl, add the paprika and season well. Add the diced butter and rub into the flour until the mixture resembles breadcrumbs. Combine 5 tablespoons of the milk with the vinegar and make a well in the middle of the flour mixture. Add the liquid and mix with a knife until the dough starts to come together, adding a drop more milk if needed. Very lightly knead the dough until smooth, flatten into a disc, wrap in cling film [plastic wrap] and chill for at least 20 minutes.

Divide the pastry in half and roll out one half on a lightly floured work surface to a thickness of about 2mm [¹⁄₁₆in]. Using a cutter or saucer as a guide, cut out 13–14-cm [5–5½-in] rounds. Gather any scraps or off-cuts together into a ball and re-roll and cut out more rounds. Repeat with the second half of the dough; you should get 12 pastry rounds in total.

Lay the pastry rounds on the work surface and divide the beef mixture between them, allowing roughly 1 heaped tablespoon per empanada and spooning the mixture neatly into the middle of the round. Brush the edges of

continued »

continued »

the pastry with milk and fold the pastry over to make neat semi-circles. Pinch the edges together to seal, brush with milk and crimp the edges decoratively between your fingers. Arrange the empanadas on a parchment-lined baking sheet.

Beat 1 tablespoon milk with the egg, brush over the tops of the empanadas and chill for 20 minutes while you preheat the oven to 180°C/350°F/Gas 4.

Meanwhile, prepare the chimichurri. Tip the garlic, shallot, chilli, herbs, vinegar and sea salt flakes into the bowl of a food processor and pulse until combined and finely chopped. Add the olive oil and lemon juice and stir to combine. Pour into a bowl, cover and set aside until ready to serve.

Brush the empanadas again with egg wash and bake on the middle shelf of the preheated oven for 20–25 minutes until the pastry is cooked, golden brown and the filling hot.

Serve the empanadas hot, fresh from the oven, or warm, with the herby chimichurri sauce alongside.

SAUSAGE & QUAIL'S EGG PIES

My other half is extremely partial to Scotch eggs, sausage rolls and pork pie. This is a mini version of all three. Crumbly, nutty pastry and nestled inside each pie sits a quail's egg surrounded by herby sausage meat. If it's in season and you're lucky enough to get hold of some, add some finely chopped wild garlic leaves to the sausage meat in place of the parsley and sage.

Pastry

200g [1½ cups] plain [all-purpose] flour, plus extra for rolling out
75g [½ cup] wholemeal spelt flour
175g [¾ cup plus 1 tsp] unsalted butter, chilled and diced
½ tsp English mustard powder
½ tsp cayenne pepper
2 tsp poppy seeds, plus extra for sprinkling
3 Tbsp ice-cold water
1 tsp cider vinegar or white wine vinegar
2 Tbsp milk
salt and freshly ground black pepper

Filling

12 quail's eggs, at room temperature
500g [1lb 2oz] good-quality sausage meat
6 spring onions [scallions], finely chopped
1 garlic clove, very finely chopped
2 rounded tsp Dijon mustard
2 Tbsp chopped flat-leaf parsley
2 tsp chopped sage

You will need a 12-hole muffin tin, preferably non-stick; an 11-cm [4½-in] plain round cutter; a 7-cm [2¾-in] plain round cutter

Makes 12

To make the pastry, combine the flours in a bowl and add a good pinch each of salt and black pepper. Add the diced butter and rub it in, first using a round-bladed or palette knife and then your hands until there are only small flecks of butter still visible.

Add the mustard powder, cayenne and poppy seeds and mix to combine. Make a well in the middle of the mixture and add the water and vinegar. Start mixing using the knife again and, once the mixture starts to form clumps, gently bring the dough together using your hands – trying not to overwork the pastry. Knead lightly for 30 seconds and then flatten into a disc, cover with cling film [plastic wrap] and chill for at least 1 hour until firm.

Meanwhile, prepare the filling. Bring a small pan of water to the boil and gently lower in the quail's eggs. Cook for exactly 2 minutes and then quickly drain and refresh the eggs under cold running water until they are completely cold. Drain and chill until needed.

Tip the sausage meat into a bowl. Add the spring onions, garlic, mustard, chopped herbs and plenty of seasoning, and mix well to combine.

Lightly dust the work surface with plain flour and divide the pastry into two portions, one piece twice a big as the other. Roll the larger piece out to a thickness of 2mm

continued »

continued »

[$^1/_{16}$ in] and, using the larger cutter, stamp out as many rounds as you can from the pastry. Gather up any scraps and off-cuts, re-roll and stamp out more rounds until you have 12. Line the muffin tin cups with these rounds.

Roll out the second piece of pastry and stamp out 12 rounds with the smaller cutter – these will be the pie lids.

Carefully peel the quail's eggs, trying to keep them intact. Divide half of the sausage meat between the pastry cases and nestle one egg into each. Gently cover the eggs with more sausage meat, mounding it up slightly in the middle of each pie.

Brush the edges of each pastry lid with milk and lay one onto each pie, pressing the edges to seal. Make a small hole in the top of each pie using the rounded end of a wooden skewer and chill the pies while you preheat the oven to 190°C/375°F/Gas 5.

Brush the top of the pies with milk, sprinkle over some poppy seeds and bake on the middle shelf of the oven for about 30 minutes until the pastry is crisp and golden.

Leave to cool slightly in the tins before removing and serving at room temperature or taking along to a picnic for some top-notch al fresco fare.

VIETNAMESE PORK PUFFS

Or to give them their real name, Bánh Pâté Sô or Pâté Chaud. These little savoury puff-pastry pies are filled with all the delicious things you'd expect to see in a spring roll, but the French influence in Vietnam is evident here in the use of puff pastry.

I have used pork in the filling but you could use chicken or turkey if you prefer, and perhaps add a handful of softened vermicelli rice noodles.

10g [⅓oz] dried shiitake
   mushrooms
350g [¾lb] minced [ground] pork
4 spring onions [scallions],
   finely sliced
2 Tbsp chopped coriander
   [cilantro]
2 garlic cloves, very finely
   chopped
2 tsp very finely chopped
   fresh ginger
2 tsp very finely chopped
   lemongrass
1 red chilli, deseeded and
   finely chopped
1 Tbsp fish sauce
1 Tbsp soy sauce
2 tsp cornflour [cornstarch]
500g [1lb 2oz] all-butter puff
   pastry (see page 12 for
   homemade)
plain [all-purpose] flour,
   for rolling out
1 egg, beaten, for sealing
   and glazing
1 Tbsp black sesame seeds
ground white pepper

Dipping sauce (optional)
juice of 2 limes
2 Tbsp palm or soft light brown
   sugar
3 Tbsp fish sauce
1 small red chilli, finely chopped

You will need a 6.5-cm [2½-in]
   square cutter and a 7-cm
   [2¾-in] square cutter

Makes 20

Start by soaking the dried shiitake mushrooms in a small bowl of boiling water for 20 minutes to soften and rehydrate. Drain, pat dry on kitchen paper [paper towels] and finely chop.

Tip the pork into a bowl and add the chopped shiitake. Add the spring onions to the pork with the chopped coriander, garlic, ginger and lemongrass. Add the chilli to the bowl with the fish sauce, soy sauce and cornflour. Season with a good pinch of ground white pepper and mix well to thoroughly combine.

Divide the pastry in half (it's easier to work with smaller amounts), and roll out on a lightly floured surface to a neat square with a thickness of 2mm [1/16in]. Using the cutters, stamp out 10 small squares and 10 larger ones and place the smaller squares on a baking sheet lined with baking parchment. Roll the pork mixture into walnut-sized balls and place one in the middle of each small square. Brush around the larger pastry squares with beaten egg and place on top of the smaller ones, egg side down and pressing the edges together to seal. Repeat with the remaining pastry and filling. Chill the pastries for 30 minutes while you preheat the oven to 190°C/375°F/Gas 5.

Meanwhile, prepare the dipping sauce, if using, by combining all the ingredients in a bowl, mixing well to dissolve the sugar. Cover and set aside.

Brush the top of the pastries with beaten egg, cut a little steam hole in the top of each and sprinkle with black sesame seeds. Bake for 30 minutes until the pastry is crisp and golden brown and the filling is piping hot. Serve hot with the dipping sauce, if using (or sriracha).

PRAWN & CRAB CURRY PUFFS

Ideal party nibbles or to serve as part of a selection of starters at an Indian dinner... either way, serve these bite-sized pastries with some mango chutney, minted yogurt raita or lime wedges to squeeze over.

2 banana [echalion] shallots, finely chopped
1 Tbsp sunflower oil
1 fat garlic clove, crushed
2 tsp grated fresh ginger
1 green or red chilli, finely chopped
½ tsp cumin seeds, coarsely ground
½ tsp fenugreek seeds, coarsely ground
½ tsp black mustard seeds
4–5 dried curry leaves, crumbled
2–3 tsp tamarind paste
1 rounded Tbsp chopped coriander [cilantro]
175g [6¼oz] raw, peeled king prawns [shrimp], deveined
100g [3½oz] picked white crabmeat
400g [14oz] all-butter puff pastry (see page 12 for homemade, and use a generous ½ quantity)
plain [all-purpose] flour, for rolling out
1 Tbsp milk
1 egg, beaten
salt and freshly ground black pepper

You will need a 10-cm [4-in] plain round cutter

Makes 20

Tip the shallots into a frying pan with the sunflower oil and cook over a medium heat until soft but not coloured. Add the garlic, ginger and chilli and cook for a further minute. Add the ground cumin and fenugreek seeds to the pan with the mustard seeds and crumbled curry leaves. Cook for a further minute until the spices smell aromatic then tip out of the pan into a bowl, add the tamarind paste and chopped coriander, season with salt and black pepper and leave to cool.

Rinse the prawns under cold water and pat dry on kitchen paper [paper towels]. Finely chop and add with the crab to the spicy onion mixture, and mix to combine.

Dust the work surface with flour and roll out the pastry to a thickness of no more than 2mm [¹/₁₆in]. Using the cutter (or a saucer as a guide) stamp out as many rounds as you can from the pastry. Gather any larger off-cuts together and stack them on top of each other. Roll out again and cut out more rounds – you should get about 20 in total.

Lay the pastry rounds on the work surface and spoon a heaped teaspoon of the cooled spiced prawn mix into the middle of each. Brush around the edge of one side of the pastry with milk and fold the pastry over the prawn mixture to completely encase the filling and make a half-moon shape. Press the edges together to seal, repeat with the remaining pastries and arrange on a baking sheet lined with baking parchment. Add the beaten egg to any remaining milk and brush over the top of each pastry. Chill the pastries for 30 minutes while you preheat the oven to 190°C/375°F/Gas 5.

Brush the pastries again with egg wash, cut a little steam hole in the top of each and bake on the middle shelf of the oven for 20–25 minutes until the pastry is crisp and golden brown. Serve hot or warm, with either some mango chutney or minty yogurt raita.

VENISON & PHEASANT PIES WITH PORCINI, CHESTNUT & CRANBERRIES

Assembling these pies is a little project – part craft and part cooking – and is an hour well spent in my opinion. Please don't skip the instruction to oil the moulds and to cover them in cling film – I did and the results weren't pretty and my language was unladylike. I find the best results are when I use straight-sided hi-ball glasses, tumblers, jam jars or ramekins.

15g [½oz] dried porcini
  mushrooms
6 Tbsp boiling water
1 oven-ready pheasant
200g [7oz] venison
50g [1¾oz] pancetta or smoked
  streaky bacon
150g [5¼oz] sausage meat
50g [1¾oz] cooked chestnuts,
  roughly chopped
50g [⅓ cup] pistachios, roughly
  chopped
50g [⅓ cup] dried cranberries
1 shallot, finely chopped
1 garlic clove, crushed
2 Tbsp chopped flat-leaf parsley
1 Tbsp chopped sage
2 Tbsp sherry or Madeira
a grating of nutmeg
125ml [½ cup] chicken stock
salt and freshly ground
  black pepper

Hot-water crust pastry
300g [2¼ cups] plain [all-purpose]
  flour, plus a little extra for
  rolling out
250g [1¾ cups] strong white flour
½ tsp caster [granulated] sugar
150g [⅔ cup] lard, diced
50g [3½ Tbsp] unsalted butter,
  diced
200ml [generous ¾ cup] water
2 medium eggs, beaten
1 Tbsp milk, for glazing
a good pinch of sea salt flakes,
  crushed
freshly ground black pepper

You will need 12 straight-sided
  glass tumblers/ramekins/jam
  jars with a base measurement
  of 5.5–6cm [2¼–2½in], and
  a 6–7-cm [2½–2¾-in] plain
  round cutter

Makes 12

Prepare the filling at least 2 hours before you plan to
assemble the pies – the day before would be even better.
This allows plenty of time for all the flavours to marry.

Soak the porcini mushrooms in the boiling water and
set aside for 30 minutes to soak and rehydrate. Cut the
breasts away from the pheasant and remove the skin and
pick out any shot. Cut as much meat off the thigh as you
can. (The remaining pheasant and carcass can be made
into stock or soup.) Cut the pheasant breast and thigh,
venison and pancetta into small pieces, about the size
of a pea, and tip into a bowl with the sausage meat. Add
the chopped chestnuts and pistachios to the bowl with
the dried cranberries. Drain the porcini and pat dry on
kitchen paper [paper towels]. Finely chop the porcini
and add to the meat with the shallot, garlic, parsley and
sage. Add the sherry or Madeira, season really well with
salt, black pepper and a grating of nutmeg and mix to
thoroughly combine the ingredients. Cover and chill
until needed.

For the hot-water crust pastry, mix the flours, sugar, salt
and black pepper in a large bowl and make a well in the
middle. Place the lard, butter and water in a small pan
and set over a medium heat. Allow the lard and butter
to melt in the water and bring to the boil. Roughly mix
three-quarters of the beaten egg into the flour, add the
hot-water mixture and, working quickly, mix the dough
together until smooth. Cover with a clean tea towel and
set aside for 20 minutes while you prepare the moulds.

Using a little sunflower oil, grease the base and sides of
the tumblers, ramekins or jars. Wrap the bases and sides
of each mould with cling film [plastic wrap], lightly oil and
set aside. Cut a sheet of baking parchment into 12 strips
– each 2–3cm [¾–1¼in] wide and long enough to wrap
around the circumference of your moulds.

continued »

SAVOURY

151

continued »

Cut off one-quarter of the hot-water crust pastry, cover and set aside – this is for the pie lids. Lightly dust the work surface with flour and divide the remaining dough into 12 pieces. Knead the first piece lightly to smooth, then roll into a round about 5mm [¼in] thick. Press the round on the cling film-covered base of the mound and use your hands to smooth the pastry over the edge and up the sides of the mould; the pastry should be of even thickness all over and should have a depth of at least 4cm [1½in] – try to make this as neat and even as possible. Repeat to make 12 pie moulds. Place on a tray and chill for 30 minutes or until firm.

Turn the mould the right way up, wrap a parchment strip around the base of the pastry and secure with string. Carefully pull the mould and cling film out of the pastry cases, which should now be pretty solid and free-standing. Divide the meat mixture into 12, shape into balls and gently press into the pastry shells, levelling the top and filling the pastry shells to within about 5mm [¼in] of the top of the pastry. Add 2 teaspoons of the chicken stock to each pie.

Roll out the remaining dough on a lightly floured surface to a thickness of about 3mm [⅛in] and, using the cutter, stamp out 12 rounds for the pie lids. Brush the edges of each round with a little water, lay on top of the meat filling and press the lids to the pastry sides to seal. Neaten up the top edge with scissors if necessary and crimp between your fingers. Push a hole

into the middle of each pie with a wooden skewer, brush the top with milk and chill on a baking sheet lined with baking parchment while you preheat the oven to 190°C/375°F/Gas 5.

Bake the pies on the middle shelf of the oven for 25 minutes then lower the oven temperature to 170°C/330°F/Gas 3½ and continue to cook for a further 20–25 minutes until the pastry is crisp and golden and the filling piping hot.

Remove the parchment and string and serve the pies hot, warm or at room temperature, with a good dollop of chutney, cranberry sauce or piccalilli.

CHEESE & ONION TARTLETS

Cheese and onion are surely a marriage made in heaven. These tarts are just enough for a couple of (slightly messy) bites and would be ideal served early evening with a refreshing glass of something chilled.

You will need onions that are neither too big nor too small, for the perfect size tartlet – so just your regular brown onions. You could serve these with an extra spoonful of pickle on the side if the mood takes you.

Rosemary & Parmesan pastry

150g [1 cup plus 2 Tbsp] plain [all-purpose] flour, plus extra for rolling out

a good pinch each of salt and freshly ground black pepper

75g [⅓ cup] unsalted butter, chilled and diced

25g [⅓ cup] finely grated Parmesan

3 tsp finely chopped rosemary or thyme leaves

about 2 Tbsp ice-cold water

1 tsp cider vinegar or white wine vinegar

Roast onions

5 medium onions

2 Tbsp olive oil

2 tsp golden caster [granulated] sugar

2 tsp balsamic or sherry vinegar

2–3 tsp thyme leaves

salt and freshly ground black pepper

Cheese sauce

15g [1 Tbsp] unsalted butter

2 tsp plain [all-purpose] flour

a good pinch of mustard powder

a pinch of cayenne pepper

200ml [generous ¾ cup] milk

75g [¾ cup] grated Cheddar

You will need a 7–8-cm [2¾–3¼-in] plain round cutter and 2 x 12-hole bun tins

Makes 20

Prepare the rosemary and Parmesan pastry using the ingredients on this page and following the instructions on page 14. Chill for at least 1 hour.

Preheat the oven to 180°C/350°F/Gas 4.

To make the roast onions, peel the onions and cut into 1-cm [³/₈-in] thick slices from stalk to root, keeping the slices and rings intact. Drizzle half of the olive oil over a baking sheet and arrange the onion slices on top in a single layer. Drizzle with more olive oil and season with half of the sugar and some salt and black pepper. Cook on the middle shelf of the oven for 20 minutes then, using a palette knife, turn the slices over, trying to keep them intact, sprinkle with more sugar and roast for a further 20 minutes. Drizzle the vinegar over the onion slices and return to the oven for a further 5 minutes, by which time they should be tender and just caramelized. Leave to cool.

While the onions are cooking, roll out the pastry on a lightly floured surface to a thickness of about 2mm [¹/₁₆in] and, using the cutter, stamp out as many rounds as you can. Gather the off-cuts together, press into a ball and roll out again – you should get 20 rounds in total. Press the rounds into the bun tins and chill until ready to bake.

To make the cheese sauce, melt the butter in a small saucepan over a low–medium heat, add the flour, mustard powder and cayenne and stir well to combine. Cook over a medium heat for a minute, until the flour starts to smell biscuity, and then slowly add the milk, whisking constantly until thoroughly incorporated. Bring the sauce to a gentle simmer and cook, stirring often, for 5 minutes until thickened and glossy. Add the grated cheese, mix to melt and combine over a low heat, remove from the heat and cool to room temperature.

Spoon the cheese sauce into the pastry cases and top with the onion slices, scatter with thyme and bake on the middle shelf of the oven for 20 minutes until the pastry is golden and the filling bubbling hot. Serve warm with perhaps a small dollop of chutney on top of each.

SAVOURY

155

BOUREKAS

Bourekas are savoury hand pies made with either puff pastry or filo and are a popular snack all across Eastern Europe and Israel. They are more often than not filled with salty cheese such as feta, greens and herbs and sometimes minced lamb or potatoes.

Here's a classic example of my indecision – I couldn't make my mind up which filling or shape of these pastries I liked best – so I've given you two. Had space allowed I would have included a third filling recipe of smoked aubergine with feta and walnuts but I will save it for another time...

You will need DOUBLE this quantity if you make both varieties of filling

375g [13¼oz] all-butter puff pastry (see page 12 for homemade, and use ½ quantity)

plain [all-purpose] flour, for rolling out

1 medium egg, beaten, for glazing

2 tsp sesame seeds

2 tsp black sesame or black onion seeds

Spinach, feta & herb filling

1 Tbsp olive oil

1 garlic clove, very finely chopped

125g [4½oz] baby leaf spinach

100g [3½oz] feta cheese

75g [⅓ cup] ricotta or cream cheese

50g [½ cup] toasted walnuts, chopped

4 spring onions [scallions], chopped

2 Tbsp chopped flat-leaf parsley

2 Tbsp chopped dill

1 mild green chilli, finely chopped

½ tsp sumac

salt and freshly ground black pepper

Makes 16–18 if you make both varieties

ingredients continued »

To make the spinach, feta and herb filling, heat the olive oil in a frying pan over a medium heat, add the garlic and cook for 20 seconds before adding the spinach. Stirring constantly, cook until the spinach has wilted then drain on a plate lined with kitchen paper [paper towels].

Roughly chop the spinach, tip into a bowl, crumble in the feta and add the ricotta, walnuts, spring onions and herbs. Add the chopped chilli, sumac and season with salt and black pepper. Mix well to combine.

Divide one quantity of the pastry in half (it's easier to work with a smaller piece). Roll out the pastry on a floured surface into a neat rectangle about 45cm [18in] long and 18–20cm [7–8in] wide and to a thickness of 1–2mm [1/16in]. Starting at one of the shorter ends, spoon one eighth of the spinach filling into a 18-cm [7-in] long cigar/sausage shape at the end of the pastry, brush the other side of the filling with water and roll the pastry over to encase and seal in the filling as if you were making sausage rolls. Cut the spinach cigar from the pastry, tuck the ends underneath, shape into a loose coil and place on a baking sheet lined with baking parchment. Repeat with the remaining filling and pastry. Brush all the bourekas with beaten egg and chill while you preheat the oven to 190°C/375°F/Gas 5.

Brush the bourekas with egg again, sprinkle with sesame and black onion seeds and bake on the middle shelf of the oven for about 35 minutes until the pastry is golden and crisp. Leave to cool slightly before serving.

continued »

continued »

Roast squash & chard filling
250g [8¾oz] peeled and diced
    butternut squash
2 Tbsp olive oil
125g [4½oz] Swiss chard
1 garlic clove, very finely chopped
100g [3½oz] feta cheese
50g [½ cup] walnuts, toasted and
    roughly chopped
1 Tbsp chopped flat-leaf parsley
1 Tbsp chopped dill
½ teaspoon sumac
salt and freshly ground
    black pepper

To make the roast squash and chard filling, preheat the oven to 190°C/375°F/Gas 5.

Tip the diced squash into a small roasting tray, toss in 1½ tablespoons of the olive oil and season with salt and black pepper. Cover loosely with foil and roast for about 20 minutes or until the squash is really tender when tested with the point of a knife. Tip into a bowl and leave to cool.

Cut the chard into ribbons, tip into a frying pan with the remaining ½ tablespoon of olive oil and the garlic, and cook over a medium heat until wilted. Tip onto a board and roughly chop. Add to the squash.

Crumble the feta into the bowl, add the walnuts, herbs and sumac and season with salt and black pepper.
Mix well to combine and to slightly break up the pieces of squash.

Roll one quantity of the pastry out on a floured surface into a neat 38-cm [15-in] square. Trim the edges to neaten and cut the pastry into 9 smaller squares, each 12cm [5in]. Spoon the filling onto the bottom right hand corner of each square. Brush the edges with water, fold the pastry squares over into triangles and press the edges to seal the filling. Arrange the pastries on a baking sheet lined with baking parchment. Brush with beaten egg and chill while you preheat the oven to 190°C/375°F/Gas 5.

Brush with egg again, snip a small steam hole in the top of each pastry, sprinkle with sesame and black onion seeds and bake on the middle shelf of the oven for about 30 minutes until the pastry is golden and crisp. Leave to cool slightly before serving.

CURRIED LAMB SAMOSAS

These samosas are baked rather than fried – so they are marginally less naughty but no less delicious. If you can, prepare the filling the day before you plan on baking and serving the samosas – this will give the spices plenty of time to mellow and I find that most curried dishes improve in flavour after 24 hours.

Curried lamb
3 shallots, roughly chopped
2 garlic cloves, roughly chopped
5-cm [2-in] piece of fresh ginger, peeled and roughly chopped
1 green chilli, deseeded and roughly chopped
1 Tbsp olive oil
500g [1lb 2oz] diced lamb shoulder
½ tsp ground coriander
½ tsp cumin seeds
½ tsp ground turmeric
½ tsp cayenne pepper
1 small cinnamon stick
3 cardamom pods, bruised
2 tomatoes, diced
½ tsp sugar
300ml [1¼ cups] lamb or light beef stock
200g [7oz] potatoes, peeled and diced
75g [½ cup] peas
2 Tbsp chopped coriander [cilantro]
salt and freshly ground black pepper

ingredients continued »

To make the curried lamb, tip the chopped shallots, garlic, ginger and chilli into a mini processor or whizzer and blend to a rough paste. Heat the olive oil in a medium, heavy-bottomed pan, add the shallot paste and cook for a few minutes until soft and aromatic but not coloured. Scoop out of the pan and set aside while you brown the lamb.

Tip the diced lamb into the pan and brown quickly over a high heat. Add the spices, stir well to coat the lamb and cook for another 30 seconds. Return the shallot paste to the pan with the diced tomatoes and sugar. Stir to combine and cook for another minute before adding the stock and seasoning well with salt and black pepper. Bring to the boil, reduce the heat to a very gentle simmer, cover and cook for about 2 hours, stirring frequently until the lamb is very tender and the sauce reduced slightly.

Add the diced potatoes and cook, uncovered, for a further 20 minutes until the potatoes are tender when tested with a knife. By now the sauce should have reduced to a rich coating consistency – if there is more than this raise the heat slightly and bubble until reduced. Add the peas and fresh coriander, check the seasoning, remove the pan from the heat and leave the curry to cool. Cover and chill until ready to bake.

continued »

continued »

Pastry
250g [1¾ cups plus 2 Tbsp] plain
[all-purpose] flour, plus extra
for rolling out
125g [1 cup] chickpea (gram) flour
½ tsp bicarbonate of soda
[baking soda]
½ tsp ground turmeric
2 tsp black onion/kalonji/nigella
seeds
½ tsp salt
100ml [⅓ cup plus 1 Tbsp]
sunflower or groundnut oil
125ml [½ cup] cold water
1½ tsp white wine (or cider)
vinegar

Makes 24

Prepare the pastry. Sift both the flours, the bicarbonate of soda and turmeric together into a large bowl. Add the black onion seeds and salt and mix to combine. Make a well in the middle of the dry ingredients, add the oil, vinegar and cold water and mix to combine using a rubber spatula and then your hands. Add a little more water if you need it to bring the dough together into a smooth ball, but do not overwork the pastry.

Return the pastry to the bowl, cover with cling film [plastic wrap] and leave to rest for 40 minutes.

Turn the dough out of the bowl and shape into 12 smooth balls, each weighing about 50g [1¾oz]. Return 6 of the balls to the bowl and keep covered while you roll out the first 6. Lightly dust the work surface with plain flour and roll out one ball into a neat round with a 17-cm [6¾-in] diameter. Using a 16-cm [6½-in] saucer or bowl as a guide, cut the pastry into a neat round, discard the trimmings and repeat this rolling and shaping for the other 5 balls of dough. Loosely cover the pastry rounds with cling film or a clean tea towel. Take one round and cut in half to make two equal semi-circles. Take one semi-circle and lightly brush the edge of the straight side with water, pick up the pastry and shape it into a cone by sticking the straight edges together, slightly overlapping and with the corners meeting. Press to seal.

Spoon a dessertspoonful of the filling into the cone, lightly brush the inside edge of one side of the open cone with water and press together to seal the filling inside. Place on a baking sheet lined with baking parchment and repeat with the remaining dough and filling.

Preheat the oven to 190°C/375°F/Gas 5 and bake for 20 minutes on the middle shelf of the oven until the pastry is crisp and turning golden at the edges, and the filling is piping hot. Serve the hot samosas with plenty of pickles and chutneys on the side.

SAVOURY

KARELIAN PIES

When I first came across these Finnish savoury pastries I was unsure – a rye-pastry shell filled with rice pudding and topped with buttery hard-boiled eggs, surely not? But they really are delicious. I have taken the unorthodox/controversial decision to serve mine with a twist of cold-smoked trout or herring and a scattering of fresh dill. I was tempted to further embellish them lightly pickled red onion… but maybe this is a step too far.

Filling
100g [½ cup] pudding (short-grain) rice
250ml [1 cup] water
½ tsp salt
600ml [2½ cups] whole milk
2 hard-boiled eggs
50g [3½ Tbsp] unsalted butter, softened
salt and freshly ground black pepper

Pastry
125g [scant 1 cup] wholemeal rye flour
75g [generous ½ cup] plain [all-purpose] or white spelt flour, plus extra for rolling out
½ tsp salt
50g [3½ Tbsp] unsalted butter, melted
125ml [½ cup] cold water

To serve
100g [3½oz] cold-smoked trout, or pickled herring
1 Tbsp chopped dill

You will need a 10–11-cm [4–4¼-in] plain round cutter or saucer

Makes 20

Start by making the filling. Tip the rice into a saucepan, add the water and salt and bring to the boil. Reduce the heat to a simmer and cook for 5 minutes. Add the milk to the pan and continue to cook gently for about 35 minutes until the rice is tender and has absorbed most of the milk. Remove from the heat, season and leave to cool

Preheat the oven to 200°C/400°F/Gas 6.

To make the pastry, combine both flours in a bowl and add the salt. Make a well in the middle of the dry ingredients, add half the melted butter and the water, and mix well, first using a palette knife and then your hands, to combine and bring the ingredients together into a neat, smooth ball. Weigh the dough and divide into 20 evenly sized pieces. Lightly dust the work surface with flour, roll each dough portion into a thin round with a thickness of no more than 2mm [¹/₁₆in] and, using the cutter or saucer as a guide, stamp out a neat round from each piece.

Lay the pastry rounds on the work surface, brush with the remaining melted butter and flip them over. Spoon the cool rice mixture in a neat mound in the middle of each round, leaving a 2-cm [¾-in] pastry border all around. Gather the pastry border in and around the rice to form a little boat-shaped tart, leaving the rice exposed. Pinch the dough edges between your fingers into little pleats, brush the rice with a little more butter and place the pies on a baking sheet lined with baking parchment. Bake on the middle shelf of the oven for 15–20 minutes until the pastry is crisp and the rice filling has just started to brown.

Chop the hard-boiled eggs, mix with the softened butter and season. Spoon on top of each pie and serve with smoked trout, or herring, and a sprinkling of chopped dill.

SLOW-COOKED BEEF SHORT RIB & MUSHROOM PIES

The filling for these spectacular pies will take 4–5 hours of oven cooking time – but very little of your attention. Ditto the pastry – which you might as well make yourself seeing as you'll have 4 hours to kill. The ingredients quantities given below are the total amounts needed for 8 pastries. If you only want 4 pastries then make only one batch of pastry but the full quantity of filling – the leftover filling will freeze for another time.

Filling
15g [½oz] dried porcini mushrooms
150ml [2/3 cup] boiling water
1 whole garlic bulb
75g [2¾oz] diced pancetta
2 Tbsp olive oil
2 onions, thinly sliced
2 garlic cloves, sliced
1.25kg [2½lb] beef short ribs (about 4 pieces)
500ml [generous 2 cups] beef stock
200ml [generous ¾ cup] red wine
1 bay leaf
1 sprig of thyme
1–2 tsp aged balsamic vinegar
125g [4½oz] chestnut button mushrooms
75g [2¾oz] chanterelle mushrooms
25g [1¾ Tbsp] unsalted butter
salt and freshly ground black pepper

Puff pastry: you will need DOUBLE this quantity
250g [1 cup plus 2 Tbsp] unsalted butter, chilled
150g [1 cup plus 2 Tbsp] plain [all-purpose] flour, plus extra for rolling out
100g [¾ cup minus ½ Tbsp] strong white flour
a pinch of salt
1 medium egg yolk, plus 1 extra egg for glazing
100–125ml [6–8 Tbsp] ice-cold water
1 tsp lemon juice or white wine vinegar

Makes 8

To make the filling, soak the dried porcini in the boiling water for 10 minutes to soften and rehydrate.

Preheat the oven to 180°C/350°F/Gas 4. Wrap the whole garlic bulb in foil and roast in the oven for 30 minutes until the cloves are tender. Squeeze out the roasted flesh from the skins and mix to a purée, then set aside. Reduce the oven temperature to 140°C/275°F/Gas 1.

While the garlic is roasting, tip the pancetta into a large, solid, lidded flameproof casserole, add half the olive oil and set the pan over a low–medium heat. Add the onions and cook with the pancetta for about 10 minutes until the onions are soft and just starting to caramelize at the edges. Add the sliced garlic to the pan and cook for a further minute.

Drain the porcini, reserving the soaking liquid. Add the porcini to the onion mixture and sauté for a minute or so.

In a large frying pan, heat the remaining olive oil until very hot, season the beef ribs, add to the pan and brown well on all sides. Place the ribs in the onion pan, add the porcini soaking liquid, stock and red wine. Add the bay leaf and thyme, season well with salt and black pepper and bring slowly to the boil. Stir well to combine, cover with a lid and cook in the middle of the oven for 2 hours.

continued »

continued »

Meanwhile, prepare TWO BATCHES of the puff pastry using the ingredients on the previous page and following the instructions on page 12.

Stir the contents of the casserole, cover and return to the oven for a further 2½ hours until the meat is really tender and falling off the bone. Remove the beef rib bones and herbs and pour the contents of the pan into a colander set over a large bowl to catch the cooking liquor. Leave the cooking liquor to settle for 20 minutes or so and for all the excess fat to rise to the top. Look over the beef and pick out and remove any pieces of gristle or tendon from the meat, then lightly shred the meat.

Carefully spoon off the excess fat and pour the cooking liquor back into the casserole, bring to the boil over a medium–high heat and continue to cook until reduced to 400ml [1²/₃ cups]. Add the balsamic vinegar to taste, and more seasoning as needed.

Meanwhile, trim the chestnut mushrooms, cut into thin slices and brush any grit from the chanterelles. Melt the butter in a frying pan, add the chestnut mushrooms, season well and cook until tender and starting to brown. Add the chanterelles and continue to cook until tender. Add to the beef and mix to combine. Leave until cold and then cover and chill until needed.

Lightly dust the work surface with flour and divide the pastry into 8 even pieces. Take one piece of pastry and cut into two – one piece slightly larger than the other. Roll the smaller piece out to a thickness of about 2mm [¹/₁₆in] and, using a saucer or small bowl as a guide, cut out a disc with a diameter of 16cm [6in]. Roll the larger piece out and cut out an 18-cm [7-in] round. Repeat with the remaining 7 pieces of pastry.

Lay the smaller rounds out on the work surface, spread the middle of each with a little roast garlic purée. Spoon the beef filling into the middle of each round, leaving a border of 1cm [³/₈in] all around. Brush the edges with water and lay the larger pastry rounds on top, pressing around the edges to seal. Using a small, sharp knife knock up the pastry around the edges (see page 135), arrange on baking sheets lined with baking parchment and chill for at least 20 minutes or until ready to bake. Preheat the oven to 190°C/375°F/ Gas 5.

Crimp the edges of each pie, brush with beaten egg and, with a wooden skewer, push a small steam hole into the top of each. Using the point of a small, sharp knife, score a decorative pattern into the top of each, cutting into but not through the pastry. Bake for 25–30 minutes until the filling is piping hot and the pastry is puffed, crisp and golden brown. Serve hot!

GOAT'S CHEESE &
COURGETTE FILO PARCELS

An exotic little hand pie – and a very tasty little snack if ever there was one. Use a soft, creamy but slightly crumbly, rindless goat's cheese that has a mild, almost grassy flavour.

Serve these pastries as soon as they are baked, when the filo will be crisp and the filling hot.

2 medium courgettes [zucchini]
4 spring onions [scallions], trimmed and finely sliced
1 small preserved lemon, rind only
1 fat garlic clove, very finely chopped
2 Tbsp chopped dill
2 Tbsp chopped mint
½ tsp cumin seeds
½ tsp ground coriander
175g [6¼oz] soft, rindless goat's cheese
10 sheets of filo [phyllo] pastry
50g [3½ Tbsp] unsalted butter, melted
1 Tbsp za'tar or sesame seeds
freshly ground black pepper

Makes 14

Coarsely grate the courgette and spread out on a double thickness of kitchen paper [paper towels], press another double layer of kitchen paper on top and leave for 45 minutes to dry off any excess moisture.

Preheat the oven to 190°C/375°F/Gas 5.

Tip the spring onions into a bowl along with the dried, grated courgette. Very finely slice the rind of the preserved lemon (discard the soft flesh), add the rind to the bowl with the garlic, chopped herbs and spices. Crumble in the goat's cheese, season with black pepper and mix well to combine.

Lay one sheet of filo on the work surface with one of the long sides nearest to you, and brush with melted butter. Top with another filo sheet. Cut into 4 vertical strips, each about 8cm [3¼in] wide, and place 1 tablespoon of the goat's cheese filling in the top right hand corner of each strip. Brush the strips with butter and fold the filling over and down the strip to encase the filling in pastry and to create neat, triangular parcels. Place on a baking sheet lined with baking parchment and repeat until the filling has been used up.

Brush the pastries with more butter, sprinkle with za'tar or sesame seeds and bake on the middle shelf of the oven for 15–20 minutes until crisp and golden. Serve immediately.

ROAST ONION, SMOKED BACON & GRUYERE TARTS

For these tarts (and for the best breakfast) it's really worth tracking down smoked bacon in one piece from your butcher – it will have much more flavour and be less watery than any pre-packed bacon.

Pastry

250g [1¾ cups plus 2 Tbsp] plain [all-purpose] flour
a good pinch each of salt and freshly ground black pepper
125g [½ cup plus 1 Tbsp] unsalted butter, chilled and diced
4 Tbsp ice-cold water
1 tsp cider vinegar or white wine vinegar

Filling

4 onions
2 Tbsp olive oil
200g [7oz] rindless smoked streaky bacon, preferably in one piece
½ tsp caster [granulated] sugar
4 medium eggs plus 3 medium yolks
375ml [generous 1½ cups] double [heavy] cream
75g [¾ cup] grated Gruyère, Comté or Cheddar
salt and freshly ground black pepper

You will need 8 x 10-cm [4-in] tart tins, 3cm [1¼in] deep

Makes 8

Prepare the pastry using the ingredients on this page and following the instructions for the Rosemary and Parmesan Pastry on page 14, leaving out the rosemary and Parmesan. Chill for at least 1 hour.

Preheat the oven to 180°C/350°F/Gas 4.

Meanwhile, for the filling, halve and peel the onions, slice off the root end and cut each half in half again through the root. Roughly separate out the layers into petals and scatter into a roasting tray. Drizzle with the oil, season with salt and black pepper and mix to combine. Loosely cover with foil and roast on the middle shelf of the oven for about 30 minutes.

Cut the bacon into dice or lardons, add to the onions with the sugar and roast, uncovered, for a further 30–35 minutes, stirring from time to time until the onions are caramelized and the bacon is crisp. Set aside until needed.

While the onions are cooking, line the tart tins. Lightly dust the work surface with flour, divide the chilled pastry into 8 evenly sized pieces and roll each piece out into a neat round with a thickness of about 3mm [⅛in]. Line the tart tins with the pastry, pressing it neatly into the corners, and trim any excess from the top. Prick the bases with a fork and pop in the fridge to rest for 20 minutes.

Meanwhile, break the eggs and yolks into a jug, add the cream, season well and whisk until thoroughly combined.

Line the chilled pastry cases with foil and fill with baking rice, place on a baking sheet and blind bake on the middle shelf of the oven for about 18 minutes until starting to turn golden at the top edge. Remove the foil and rice and bake for a further minute or two to dry out the bases. Reduce the oven temperature to 170°C/330°F/Gas 3½.

Divide the grated cheese, roasted onions and bacon between each tart shell, and pour over the egg mixture to fill. Return to the oven and bake for 25 minutes until the filling is golden and just set. Serve warm with a crisp green salad.

CORNISH PASTIES

Reminiscent of wind-swept beaches and sandy toes – there's a good
reason why most Cornish seaside towns have numerous pasty shops with
queues of tourists (and locals) snaking out of the door.

Serve with tomato ketchup or brown sauce, or both.

Pastry
200g [1½ cups] plain [all-purpose]
  flour, plus extra for rolling out
300g [2 cups plus 2 Tbsp] strong
  white flour
100g [½ cup minus 1 Tbsp] lard,
  chilled and diced
75g [⅓ cup] unsalted butter,
  chilled and diced
about 150ml [⅔ cup] ice-cold
  water
½ tsp white wine vinegar, cider
  vinegar or lemon juice
salt and freshly ground
  black pepper
1–2 Tbsp milk, for glazing

Filling
300g [10½oz] stewing steak,
  ideally skirt or bavette
250g [8¾oz] waxy potatoes, peeled
150g [5¼oz] peeled swede
  [rutabaga]
1 onion (about 150g/5¼oz
  when peeled)
1–2 Tbsp beef stock
a dash of Worcestershire sauce
  (they'll never let me back in
  Cornwall again)
75g [⅓ cup] butter (preferably
  Cornish clotted cream butter)

Makes 6

Start by making the pastry. Tip both flours into a large
mixing bowl, add the diced lard and butter and a good
pinch each of salt and black pepper. Using a palette or
round-bladed knife, cut the fats into the flours until the
pieces are half their original size. Then switch to using
your hands to rub the fats into the flour.

When there are only very small flecks of fat still visible,
make a well in the middle of the mixture, add 150ml
[⅔ cup] ice-cold water and the vinegar and mix again
using the knife. When the mixture starts to clump
together, switch back to using your hands to gather
and press the dough together into a ball, adding a little
more water if needed. Knead the dough very gently for
10 seconds, flatten into a disc, cover with cling film
[plastic wrap] and chill for at least 1 hour until firm.

Meanwhile, get on with the filling. Cut the steak into
small 1–2-cm [⅜–¾-in] nuggets and tip into a bowl. Do
the same with the potato and swede – the meat, potato
and swede pieces should all be roughly the same size.
Rather than making them neat little dice, I like to hold
the potato in my left hand and then, using a small sharp
knife, cut little evenly sized chips straight into the bowl,
and then do the same with the swede. Chop the onion and
add this to the bowl along with the beef stock and some
heavy-handed seasoning. And I know that this is far from
normal, but I like to add a dash of Worcestershire sauce
too. Mix well to combine.

Dust the work surface with flour, divide the dough into
6 evenly sized portions and roll the first piece out to a
thickness of about 3mm [⅛in]. Using a side plate as a
guide, cut the pastry into a 20-cm [8-in] round, then repeat

continued »

with the remaining 5 pieces of pastry. Lay
the pastry rounds on the work surface,
divide the filling between them, mounding
it evenly onto one side of the round and
leaving a clear border, and top the filling
with a nugget of butter.

Brush the edges of the pastry with water,
fold the pastry over the filling to make
a half-moon shape and press the edges
together to seal. Crimp and fold the edges
together, arrange the pasties on a baking
sheet lined with baking parchment and
chill for 30 minutes or until ready to bake.

Preheat the oven to 190°C/375°F/Gas 5.

Brush the pasties with milk, cut a small
hole in the top of each and bake on the
middle shelf of the oven for 20 minutes.
Reduce the heat to 180°C/350°F/Gas 4 and
cook for a further 20–25 minutes until the
pastry is crisp and golden and the filling
steaming hot.

SAVOURY

FOOTBALL PIES

Half-time at football matches the length and breadth of Great Britain means one thing – hot meat pies. Some football clubs are famed for the quality of pies served and there is even a pie league table with competition as fierce as that on the pitch. This is my take on the half-time pie – the pastry is probably a little more buttery and flaky than commercially made football pies but in my mind that's no bad thing.

The filling should be prepared ahead and be completely cold (chilled is better) before assembly.

Filling
1 onion, finely chopped
1 Tbsp olive oil
1 garlic clove, crushed
500g [1lb 2oz] minced [ground] lamb or beef
1 rounded Tbsp tomato purée [paste]
2 tsp plain [all-purpose] flour
300ml [1¼ cups] beef stock
a good dash of Worcestershire sauce
1 bay leaf
1 large carrot, peeled and diced
1 red skinned potato (200g/7oz peeled weight), peeled and diced
salt and freshly ground black pepper

Pastry
400g [3 cups] plain [all-purpose] flour, plus extra for rolling out
100g [½ cup minus 1 Tbsp] lard, chilled and diced
100g [½ cup minus 1 Tbsp] unsalted butter, chilled and diced
4–5 Tbsp ice-cold water
1 tsp cider or white wine vinegar
1 Tbsp milk, for glazing

You will need 6 x 13-cm [5-in] foil pie dishes, 3cm [1¼in] deep

Makes 6

Start by making the filling so that it has plenty of time to cool down before assembling the pies. Tip the onion into a saucepan or flameproof casserole, add the olive oil and cook over a low–medium heat until the onion is soft and translucent. Add the garlic and continue to cook for another minute. Add the lamb or beef, increase the heat to high and cook quickly to brown the mince.

Add the tomato purée, stir well to combine and cook for another minute until it starts to caramelize. Add the flour, stir well, cook for another 30 seconds then add the stock, stirring well to incorporate any delicious caramelized bits that might be stuck on the bottom of the pan, and bring to the boil. Season well, add the Worcestershire sauce and the bay leaf, reduce the heat to a very gentle simmer, cover with a lid and cook for 30 minutes.

Add the carrot to the pan, cover and cook for another 10 minutes then add the diced potato and cook for a further 10–15 minutes until both are tender. By now the filling should be thickened and rich with enough gravy to coat the meat but not swamp it – if it's too sloppy, cook for a few minutes more to reduce, and if it's too dry add a little more stock.

continued »

continued »

Check the seasoning, pick out the bay leaf, remove from the heat and leave to cool. Scoop into a bowl, cover and chill until ready to assemble the pies.

To make the pastry, tip the flour into a bowl, add a good pinch each of salt and black pepper and the diced lard and butter, and rub in using first a round-bladed or palette knife and then your hands. When there are only small flecks of fat still remaining, make a well in the middle of the mixture, add the water and vinegar and cut the wet into the dry to combine. Use your hands to gather the pastry together into a neat ball, knead very briefly, flatten into a disc, cover with cling film [plastic wrap] and chill for 2 hours until firm.

Lightly dust the work surface with flour, divide the pastry into 6 equal pieces and, taking the first piece, cut it in half, with one portion twice as large as the other. Roll the larger portion out into a neat round with a thickness of about 2mm [1/16in] and use to line a foil pie dish, pressing the pastry evenly to cover the base and sides, with a little extra hanging over the top.

Spoon one-sixth of the pie filling into the pastry-lined dish and spread level with the back of a spoon. Roll the smaller portion of pastry into a neat round, large enough to cover the top of the pie. Brush the edges of the pie with water and lay the round on top to cover the filling. Pinch the edges to seal and trim off any excess pastry. Repeat with the remaining pastry and filling to make 6 pies. Cover and chill the pies until ready to cook.

Preheat the oven to 190°C/375°F/Gas 5, placing a solid baking sheet on the middle shelf to heat up.

Brush the tops of the pies with milk, make a hole in the middle of each with a wooden skewer and bake on the hot baking sheet for about 30 minutes until the filling is piping hot and the pastry golden brown and crisp.

Serve with extra gravy on the side and ketchup and brown sauce.

CHICORY & SHALLOT TART

My dog Nellie believes that whatever goes on in the kitchen is for her benefit. When I was testing this recipe I left the freshly baked tart cooling on the counter top and Nellie snoozing in her bed. On my return, less than 2 minutes later, she had scoffed the entire tart, leaving a small pile of puff pastry crumbs on the plate. It has the Nellie seal of approval.

Serve with a watercress salad dressed with a mustardy vinaigrette, a handful of toasted walnuts and nuggets of creamy blue cheese.

50g [3½ Tbsp] unsalted butter
1 Tbsp olive oil
6 banana [echalion] shallots, peeled and halved through the root from top to bottom
2 heads of chicory [endive], halved from root to tip
2 garlic cloves, thinly sliced
1 rounded Tbsp capers, drained
2 sprigs of thyme, leaves only
300g [10½oz] all-butter puff pastry (see page 12 for homemade, and use ½ quantity)
plain [all-purpose] flour, for rolling out
salt and freshly ground black pepper

You will need an ovenproof frying pan with a base measurement of 20cm [8in]

Serves 4 (or one naughty dog)

Preheat the oven to 190°C/375°F/Gas 5.

Melt the butter with the olive oil in the frying pan, add the shallots, cut side down, and cook over a medium heat for 5 minutes until starting to caramelize. Carefully remove from the pan using a palette knife, season with salt and black pepper and set aside. Add the chicory halves to the pan, cut side down, and cook for about 4 minutes until starting to turn golden and softened slightly at the edges.

Nestle the sliced garlic, capers and thyme leaves around the chicory, return the shallot halves to the pan, cut side down, and arrange around the chicory halves. Cover the pan with foil and cook on the middle shelf of the oven for 25 minutes or until the shallots and chicory have softened and are light golden. Remove the pan from the oven and increase the oven temperature to 200°C/400°F/Gas 6.

Dust the work surface with flour, roll the pastry into a neat square and cut into a 30-cm [12-in] round, using a dinner plate as a guide. Lay the pastry on top of the veggies and tuck the edges of the pastry inside the pan rather like tucking in a bed. Make a small hole in the middle of the pastry to allow steam to escape and return the pan to a medium–high heat on the hob for 1 minute, then slide the pan back into the oven and cook for a further 20–25 minutes until the pastry is puffed, crisp and deep golden.

Remove from the oven, leave the tart to rest for 2 minutes then place a serving plate on top of the pan and, with your hands safely covered with a heatproof cloth or oven gloves, quickly flip the pan over and the tart out onto the plate. Serve hot, warm or at room temperature, with a crisp green salad.

SAVOURY

175

MANCHEGO, PEAR & SERRANO HAM PASTRIES

These are quite possibly some of the tastiest and quickest party nibbles you can make – and they'll be even quicker if you use storebought all-butter puff pastry. If you want to make you own pastry (or have some knocking about in the freezer from another recipe) you will need roughly half the quantity of homemade from page 12.

300g [10½oz] all-butter puff pastry (see page 12 for homemade, and use ½ quantity)
plain [all-purpose] flour, for rolling out
200g [7oz] Manchego cheese
3 Conference pears
50g [generous ⅓ cup] pine nuts, toasted
leaves from 3 bushy thyme sprigs
8–10 slices of serrano ham
2 Tbsp clear honey

Makes 25

Roll out the puff pastry on a lightly floured surface into a neat, roughly 30-cm [12-in] square, no more than 2mm [¹/₁₆in] thick. Using a long, sharp knife trim the sides to neaten and cut the pastry into 25 neat squares. Arrange the pastry squares on parchment-lined baking sheets and chill for 20 minutes while you prepare the toppings and preheat the oven to 200°C/400°F/Gas 6.

Remove the rind from the Manchego and cut the cheese into wafer-thin slices. Quarter and core the pears and cut into very thin slices.

Arrange the Manchego and pear slices randomly on top of each pastry square and scatter over the toasted pine nuts and thyme leaves. Bake on the middle shelf of the oven for about 15 minutes until the pastry is golden and crisp and the cheese melted.

Leave to cool for 2 minutes or so then drape a twist of serrano ham on top of each pastry, drizzle with a little honey and serve immediately.

SMOKED SALMON & POACHED EGG TARTS

The rye pastry will make more than you need for these 4 tarts, but I would suggest that you make the quantity given, as I find it tricky to make small quantities of pastry. And besides, it's helpful to have some stashed in the freezer or fridge for the following weekend so that you are prepared for another weekend of brunch bliss.

Pastry with rye
175g [1⅓ cups] plain [all-purpose] flour, plus extra for rolling out
75g [scant ¾ cup] white rye flour
a pinch each of salt and freshly ground black pepper
175g [¾ cup plus 2 tsp] unsalted butter, chilled and diced
2 medium egg yolks
2 tsp cider vinegar
1–2 Tbsp ice-cold water

Filling
25g [1¾ Tbsp] unsalted butter
½ tsp dried Aleppo chilli flakes
1 tsp vinegar
1 avocado
4 Tbsp cream cheese
100g [3½oz] smoked salmon
4 eggs
a small bunch of dill, very roughly chopped
a handful of pea shoots or watercress
lemon wedges, to serve

You will need 4 x 12-cm [5-in] tart tins

Makes 4

To make the pastry, combine both flours in a large bowl and add the salt and black pepper. Add the butter and cut it into the flour using a round-bladed knife until the butter pieces are half their original size. Now switch to using your hands to continue rubbing the butter in. Lift handfuls of butter and flour up and allow it to fall back into the bowl through your fingertips, gently pressing the butter pieces between your fingers.

When there are only small flecks of butter still visible, make a well in the middle of the mixture, add the egg yolks, vinegar and 1 tablespoon of ice-cold water. Use the knife to cut the wet ingredients into the dry, adding a drop more water if necessary – the pastry should be slightly sticky rather than wet – and, when the mixture starts to clump together, use your hands to bring the dough together into a ball. Flatten into a disc, wrap in cling film [plastic wrap] and chill for at least 2 hours.

Dust the work surface with flour. You will only need half of the prepared pastry for this recipe so cut the dough in half, wrap one piece in cling film and chill for up to 1 week or freeze for 1 month. Cut the other piece into 4 evenly sized pieces and roll each out into a neat round 2–3mm [1/16–1/8in] thick. Line the tart tins with the pastry rounds and trim any excess pastry from the tops of the tins. Prick the bases with a fork and chill for 30 minutes while you preheat the oven to 180°C/350°F/Gas 4.

Line each pastry case with foil, fill with baking rice and bake on the middle shelf of the oven for about 15 minutes until the top edge of each tart shell starts to turn golden. Remove the foil and rice and continue to cook for a further couple of minutes to crisp the base. Leave to cool.

continued »

Tip the butter into a small pan, add the
Aleppo chilli flakes and season with salt
and black pepper. Gently melt the butter,
remove from the heat and leave to infuse
for 15 minutes while you prepare the rest
of the filling.

Bring a medium pan of salted water to
a simmer and add the vinegar. Peel the
avocado, halve and remove the stone and
cut into delicate slices. Lightly beat the
cream cheese until softened and smooth,
divide between the cooled pastry cases and
spread level. Fold a twist of smoked salmon
into one-third of each tart and arrange the
avocado slices in another third.

Carefully break the eggs, one at a time, into
a ramekin or tea cup and drop into the
simmering water to poach for 2 minutes
or until cooked to your liking. Meanwhile,
warm the chilli butter. Remove the poached
eggs from the pan using a slotted spoon
and drain quickly on kitchen paper [paper
towels]. Place the poached eggs in the tarts,
drizzle over the butter and sprinkle with
dill and pea shoots. Serve immediately,
with a lemon wedge on the side.

SPICED LAMB & PRUNE PIES

These pies started life as a tagine-style supper dish; the next day we had some left over along with half a pack of filo pastry that was looking for a use. We combined the two, resulting in a very successful fridge forage.

I suggest using a leg of lamb and dicing it yourself here, as pre-packed diced meat is often in smaller or irregular pieces which cook unevenly.

The ingredients list looks lengthy but is in fact mostly spices or store-cupboard ingredients.

8–10 sheets of filo [phyllo] pastry
50g [3½ Tbsp] unsalted butter, melted
1 tsp za'tar

Filling
1 tsp cumin seeds
1 tsp coriander seeds
1 tsp fennel seeds
1 tsp fenugreek seeds
½ tsp cayenne pepper
1.25–1.5kg [2½–3½lb] boned leg of lamb
2–3 Tbsp olive oil
2 large onions, sliced
3-cm [1¼-in] piece of fresh ginger, grated
3 garlic cloves, crushed
1 large red chilli, finely chopped (include the seeds for extra heat)
1 Tbsp tomato purée [paste]
600ml [2½ cups] chicken, light lamb or beef stock
1 x 400-g [14-oz] can of chopped tomatoes
1 cinnamon stick
4 cardamom pods, lightly crushed
1 bay leaf
2–3 Tbsp honey
2 tsp cider vinegar
100g [3½oz] stoned prunes, quartered
2 Tbsp chopped coriander [cilantro]
salt and freshly ground black pepper

Makes 6 individual pies

If time allows, make the filling the day before you plan on serving the pies, as the flavour will improve and the spices will mellow after it has had an overnight rest in the fridge.

Start by making the spice mix for the filling. Tip the seeds into a large, dry frying pan and toast over a medium heat for 1 minute, shaking the pan from time to time until the spices smell toasted. Grind using a pestle and mortar, add the cayenne and set aside. Do not wash the frying pan as you'll need it to brown the lamb.

Preheat the oven to 140°C/275°F/Gas 1.

Trim any excess fat and sinew from the meat the cut the lamb into 3-cm [1¼-in] chunks. Heat half of the oil in the frying pan and brown the lamb in batches over a high heat. Do not overcrowd the pan or the meat will stew rather than brown. As each batch of lamb is browned, remove it from the pan and tip into a flameproof casserole that has a lid.

When all of the meat has been browned add another tablespoon of olive oil to the frying pan, add the onions and cook gently for about 10 minutes until tender and starting to caramelize at the edges. Add the ground toasted spices, ginger, garlic and chilli and cook for a further minute or so. Add the tomato purée, mix well and cook for another minute before adding half of the stock. Stir well to incorporate any bits of deliciousness that might be stuck to the bottom of the pan. Pour the contents of the frying pan into the casserole with the lamb, add the remaining stock, tomatoes, cinnamon, cardamom, bay leaf, honey and vinegar and bring slowly

continued »

to the boil. Cover the pan with a lid and transfer to the preheated oven to slowly cook for about 3 hours, until the meat is tender and the sauce reduced.

If the mixture is still quite liquidy after this time, pop the pan over a medium heat, bring to the boil and reduce the liquid slightly. Taste and adjust the seasoning as necessary, adding a touch more honey or vinegar, salt and black pepper as needed. Remove the cinnamon stick, cardamom pods and bay leaf, add the prunes and chopped coriander and divide the filling between 6 individual pie dishes. Leave to cool and then cover and chill until ready to bake the pies.

Preheat the oven to 180°C/350°F/Gas 4.

Unwrap the filo pastry and brush each sheet with melted butter. Scrunch up the buttered pastry sheets and place on top of the pies – depending on the size of your filo pastry sheets and your pie dishes you may need 1 or 1½ sheets of pastry per pie to cover the filling. Scatter with za'tar and place the pie dishes on a baking sheet. Bake on the middle shelf of the oven for about 40 minutes until the pastry is golden and crisp and the filling is hot.

BAKED TUNWORTH

Tunworth is a soft-rinded British cheese very similar to Camembert, and is made 3 miles from where I live. Most of our local pubs have it on their menus in one form or another – baked is always hugely popular.

1 onion
3 garlic cloves, unpeeled
1 Tbsp olive oil
5g [¼oz] dried porcini
   mushrooms
1 x 250-g [8¾-oz] Tunworth
   cheese or Camembert
2 tsp thyme leaves
1 small black truffle (optional)
350g [¾lb] all-butter puff pastry
   (see page 12 for homemade,
   and use ½ quantity)
plain [all-purpose] flour,
   for rolling out
1 medium egg, beaten, for glazing
salt and freshly ground
   black pepper

Serves 4

Preheat the oven to 170°C/330°F/Gas 3½.

Peel the onion, cut into quarters and separate the layers into petals. Scatter the onion petals in a small roasting tray with the garlic, drizzle with the olive oil and roast for 40 minutes until softened and caramelized at the edges. Season and leave to cool.

Put the dried porcini mushrooms into a small heatproof bowl, add boiling water to cover and leave to soak for 10–15 minutes until soft and rehydrated. Drain the mushrooms, pat dry on kitchen paper [paper towels] and finely chop. Mix the porcini and thyme leaves into the roasted onions.

Cut the pastry into two pieces, one slightly larger than the other. Roll the smaller piece on a lightly floured surface into a round 2–3cm [¾–1¼in] wider all round than the cheese, and place on a baking sheet lined with baking parchment. Place the roasted onion and porcini mixture in the middle of the pastry round, squeeze the garlic cloves from their skins, dot the soft flesh around the onions and nestle the cheese on top. Brush the edges of the pastry with a little beaten egg.

Roll the second piece of pastry out into a round about 4–5cm [1½–2in] wider all round than the cheese and drape over the top, neatly covering the top and sides of the cheese. Gently press the pastry down to neatly encase the cheese, press the edges together to seal and trim off any excess. Using a small, sharp knife, knock up the edges of the pastry (see page 135), glaze all over with beaten egg and chill for 20 minutes while you preheat the oven to 190°C/375°F/Gas 5.

Glaze the pastry again and using the point of a small sharp knife score a decorative pattern into the pastry being careful that you don't cut all the way through. Make a steam hole in the middle of the pastry with a wooden skewer and bake on the middle shelf of the preheated oven for 20–25 minutes until the pastry is golden brown and crisp. Rest for 5 minutes and then serve with some good bread for mopping up the molten cheese.

ROAST CARROT & BEETROOT TARTS

Look out for Chantenay, smallish heritage or rainbow carrots, and smallish beetroot (no larger than a tennis ball) and candy-striped or golden beetroot when in season.

I particularly like to use sheep's milk yogurt for making labneh – it has a mild, slightly grassy and tangy flavour but any good-quality, full-fat natural yogurt will do just as well.

I have included a recipe for dukkah – a toasted and ground spice and seed seasoning to scatter over these tarts. It will make more than you need for this recipe but it will keep in a screw-top jar for other times when you need to add a lift to salads, soups or savoury tarts.

Labneh
600g [2¾ cups] full-fat plain yogurt (I like to use sheep's milk yogurt)
a pinch of sea salt

Pastry
175g [1⅓ cups] plain [all-purpose] flour, plus extra for rolling out
75g [scant ¾ cup] white rye flour
a good pinch each of salt and freshly ground black pepper
175g [¾ cup plus 1 tsp] unsalted butter, chilled and diced
2 medium egg yolks
3 tsp cider vinegar
1–2 Tbsp ice-cold water

Filling
500g [1lb 2oz] smallish beetroots [beet]
400g [14oz] small or heritage carrots
2 Tbsp olive oil
2–3 Turkish pickled green chillies, roughly chopped
2 Tbsp stoned green olives, roughly chopped
2–3 Tbsp pomegranate seeds
2 Tbsp roughly chopped dill
2 Tbsp roughly chopped parsley
2 Tbsp roughly chopped mint
1 garlic clove
extra virgin olive oil, to drizzle

You will need to make the labneh the day before you plan on serving these tarts. Tip the yogurt into a bowl, season with the sea salt and mix to combine. Scoop the yogurt into a sieve lined with a clean, new J-cloth or butter muslin [cheesecloth]. Set the sieve over a bowl, cover with cling film [plastic wrap] and chill for 24 hours to allow the yogurt to thicken and the whey to drip out.

To make the pastry, combine both flours in a large bowl and add the salt and black pepper. Add the butter and cut it into the flour using a round-bladed or palette knife until the butter pieces are half their original size. Now switch to using your hands to continue rubbing the butter in. Lift handfuls of butter and flour up and allow it to fall back into the bowl through your fingertips, gently pressing the butter pieces between your fingers.

When there are only small flecks of butter still visible, make a well in the middle of the mixture, add the egg yolks, vinegar and 1 tablespoon of ice-cold water. Use the knife to cut the wet ingredients into the dry, adding a drop more water if necessary – the pastry should be slightly sticky rather than wet – and, when the mixture starts to clump together, use your hands to bring the dough together into a ball. Flatten into a disc, wrap in cling film and chill for at least 2 hours.

ingredients continued »

continued »

Dukkah
1 Tbsp pumpkin seeds
1 Tbsp sesame seeds
2 tsp coriander seeds
2 tsp cumin seeds

You will need 8 x 12-cm
   [5-in] tart tins

Makes 8 small tarts

Dust the work surface with flour and divide the pastry into 8 equal pieces. Roll each piece out into a round 2–3mm [$^1/_{16}$–$^1/_8$in] thick and use to line the tart tins. Trim any excess from the top of each tart, prick the bases with a fork and chill for 30 minutes while you preheat the oven to 180°C/350°F/Gas 4. Line the tarts with foil, fill with baking rice and bake on the middle shelf of the oven for about 15 minutes until the top edge starts to turn golden. Remove the foil and rice and continue to cook for a further couple of minutes to crisp the base. Leave to cool.

While the oven is on, spoon all of the ingredients for the dukkah into a small roasting tray and roast for 3–4 minutes. Coarsely grind using a pestle and mortar and season with salt and black pepper.

Trim and peel the beetroot and cut each into 1-cm [$^3/_8$-in] thick wedges. Scrub the carrots and cut in half from root to stalk. Tip the beetroot into a roasting tray, drizzle with oil and season with salt and black pepper. Roast on the middle shelf of the oven for about 30 minutes then add the carrots and cook for a further 20 minutes until the veggies are tender when tested with the point of a knife.

Tip the chopped pickled chillies and olives into a bowl, add the pomegranate seeds and herbs and mix to combine.

Scoop the strained yogurt into a bowl and season. Finely grate the garlic into the bowl and mix. Divide the labneh between the baked tart shells and spread level. Arrange the veggies on top of the labneh, scatter with the herb mixture and sprinkle over a little of the dukkah. Drizzle with extra virgin olive oil and serve immediately.

SAVOURY

185

SMOKED AUBERGINE & HERB TARTS

Abandon your baking tins for these savoury tarts – these are all about simplicity, freshness and flavour. The walnut pastry is a little crumblier than regular pastry and so works well in this free-form shape.

Cooking aubergines over an open flame gives them a smoky flavour and renders the flesh to a silky tenderness. Halloumi is often fried or grilled but here I've grated it over each tart; its saltiness contrasts beautifully with the smoky aubergine, fresh herbs and sweet pomegranate seeds.

Walnut pastry
75g [²/₃ cup] walnuts
100g [¾ cup] plain [all-purpose] flour, plus extra for rolling out
100g [¾ cup] spelt flour
100g [½ cup minus 1 Tbsp] unsalted butter, chilled and diced
4 Tbsp olive oil
2 Tbsp ice-cold water
1 tsp cider vinegar
salt and freshly ground black pepper

Smoked aubergine
2 aubergines [eggplants]
1 fat garlic clove, roughly chopped
4 Tbsp Greek yogurt
2 Tbsp tahini
juice of ½ lemon

Topping
4 spring onions [scallions], finely sliced on the diagonal
8 radishes, thinly sliced
a small bunch of flat-leaf parsley, leaves only
a small bunch of coriander [cilantro], leaves only
a small bunch of mint, leaves only
a small bunch of dill, leaves only
seeds from ½ pomegranate
100g [3½oz] halloumi
2 Tbsp extra virgin olive oil
a good pinch of ground sumac

Makes 6

Start by making the walnut pastry. Tip the walnuts into a food processor or mini-chopper and whizz until finely chopped but still with a little texture. Combine the flours, season with salt and pepper, add the diced butter and rub in using your fingertips until only small flecks of butter remain. Add the walnuts and mix. Make a well in the middle of the ingredients, add the olive oil, ice-cold water and cider vinegar. Using a round-bladed or palette knife, mix to roughly combine and then switch to using your hands to gather the dough into a neat ball. Flatten the dough into a disc, cover with cling film [plastic wrap] and chill for at least 1 hour until firm.

Meanwhile, prepare the smoked aubergine. Place the whole aubergines directly over the gas flame (or barbecue if you happen to have one lit for something else). Failing that, a very hot ridged griddle pan will suffice, but whichever indoor cooking method you are using, make sure that you turn on your extractor fan… smoke alarms are noisy and upset the neighbours. Cook the aubergine over the open flame (or on the griddle pan), turning from time to time until the skin is really well charred and blackened and the flesh inside is very soft and slumped. Remove from the heat, leave to cool for a few minutes then peel off the burnt skin and scoop the flesh into a sieve set over a bowl. Leave to drain for 30 minutes or so.

continued »

continued »

Tip the garlic into a food processor with
the drained aubergine flesh and whizz
until roughly combined. Add the yogurt,
tahini and lemon juice and season with
salt and black pepper. Whizz again until
smooth, taste and add more lemon juice
or seasoning as needed. Scoop into
a bowl, cover with cling film and chill
until required.

Preheat the oven to 180°C/350°F/Gas 4.

Dust the work surface with flour, divide
the walnut pastry into 6 evenly sized pieces
and roll each out to a rough oval shape
about 3mm [⅛in] thick. Don't worry too
much about neatness – these tarts are a
little rough around the edges. Slide the
pastry ovals onto two parchment-lined
baking sheets and bake near the middle
of the oven for about 14 minutes until
just crisp and biscuity. Leave to cool
to room temperature.

Place the pastries on a board or plates and
spread with the smoked aubergine. Top
the aubergine with the herbs and sprinkle
over the sliced spring onions and radishes,
and the pomegranate seeds. Finely grate
the halloumi over each tart, drizzle with
extra virgin olive oil, season with a pinch
of sumac and serve immediately.

CHICKEN, LEEK & TARRAGON PIE

This might seem a labour of love – poaching a chicken, then reducing the liquor to make a rich, silky sauce – all to go into a pie. And that's before you've even started making your own puff pastry. But if something is worth doing it's worth doing well. So this is a pie to save for best, like those times when you need to pull out all the stops.

1 large chicken, about 1.8kg [4lb]
1 large or 2 small onions
2 celery sticks, roughly chopped
1 leek, roughly chopped
1 large/2 small carrots, chopped
2 garlic cloves, bruised
1 sprig of thyme
a handful of parsley stalks
6 black peppercorns
8 baby leeks, trimmed and cut into 2-cm [¾-in] lengths

Puff pastry
125g [1 cup minus 1 Tbsp] plain [all-purpose] flour, plus extra
125g [¾ cup plus 2 Tbsp] strong white flour
1 tsp English mustard powder
a good pinch of salt
150g [⅔ cup] unsalted butter, chilled and diced
50g [¾ cup] finely grated Parmesan
125ml [½ cup] ice-cold water
1 tsp cider vinegar
1 medium egg, beaten with 1 Tbsp milk, for glazing

Sauce
50g [3½ Tbsp] unsalted butter
50g [6 Tbsp] plain [all-purpose] flour
2 Tbsp Dijon mustard
150g [5¼oz] crème fraîche
150g [1⅓ cups] grated Gruyère
2 big Tbsp chopped tarragon
salt and ground black pepper

You will need an oval or round pie dish with a capacity of about 2 litres [2 quarts]

Serves 4–6

Start by poaching the chicken. Place the chicken in a large stockpot. Peel and halve the onions, then add to the pot with the celery, roughly chopped leek, carrots, garlic and herbs. Pour enough cold water into the pot to cover the chicken, add the peppercorns, half cover the pot with a lid and bring slowly to the boil. Simmer the chicken for about 40 minutes until just cooked, remove from the heat and leave to cool in the liquid.

While the chicken is cooling, prepare the puff pastry. Sift both flours into a large bowl, add the mustard powder and salt. Add the diced butter and Parmesan and rub in using your fingers until the butter is still in large pieces but the corners have been rounded off and the butter is well coated in flour. Add the water and vinegar and mix to combine using a round-bladed or palette knife, adding a little more water if needed to bring the dough together without over-kneading. Gather the dough into a ball, flatten into a neat rectangle, cover with cling film [plastic wrap] and chill for 20 minutes.

Lightly dust the work surface with plain flour and roll the dough out into a neat rectangle three times as long as it is wide (15 x 45cm/6 x 18in) and with one of the shorter sides nearest to you. Fold the bottom third of the rectangle up over the middle third and the bottom third down to cover. Turn the square 90° and roll out in the same way again. Fold the dough up into thirds as before, wrap in baking parchment and chill for 30 minutes.

continued »

continued »

Roll and fold the pastry twice more, wrap and chill again until ready to use.

Lift the cold chicken from the pan and strip all of the meat from the bones, keeping the pieces as large as possible, then chill until needed. Discard the skin and return the bones to the stockpot. Place the pan back on the heat, bring to the boil and simmer for 1 hour, removing any scum that rises to the surface of the stock, using a slotted spoon. Strain the stock into another pan, bring back to the boil and continue to cook until the liquid has reduced to 750ml [generous 3 cups].

For the sauce, melt the butter in a large pan, add the flour and cook for 30 seconds until it starts to smell biscuity. Gradually add the reduced stock, whisking constantly until smooth. Continue to simmer gently for 10 minutes until thickened, glossy and smooth. Add the mustard, crème fraîche, Gruyère and tarragon, mix to combine and season well with salt and black pepper. Remove from the heat and leave to cool before adding the reserved chicken.

Blanch the baby leeks in salted boiling water for 1 minute or until just tender. Drain well and pat dry on kitchen paper [paper towels]. Place a pie funnel in the pie dish and spoon the chicken and leeks into the dish around the funnel.

Lightly dust the work surface with flour and roll the pastry out to a thickness of about 3mm [1/8in], and 4cm [1½in] wider all round than your pie dish. Cut a 1–2-cm [3/8–¾-in] wide strip from the pastry and brush with water, then stick this strip – wet side down – to the rim of the dish and

brush again with water. Cut the remaining pastry into an oval or round (or whatever shape your pie dish happens to be) that is 2cm [¾in] wider all around than the pie dish, and carefully place the pastry on top of the pie, pressing to seal the edges onto the pastry strip and cutting a hole into the middle to allow the top of the funnel to poke through. Any pastry off-cuts can be shaped into leaves and arranged on top of the pie. Score the sides of the pastry with a sharp knife, crimp the edges with your fingers and brush the top of the pastry with the egg wash. Chill for 20 minutes while you preheat the oven to 180°C/350°F/Gas 4.

Brush the pastry with egg wash again, place the pie on a baking sheet and cook for about 40 minutes until the filling is piping hot and the pastry is golden, risen and crispy.

SAVOURY

MIXED TOMATO GALETTE

This is a tart to make in the height of summer when the tomatoes are at their most abundant and brilliant. Seek out tomatoes in a variety of shapes and sizes, ranging from yellow and red cherry tomatoes to yellow plums and even tiger-striped or purple-skinned.

Poppy-seed & Parmesan pastry
100g [¾ cup] plain [all-purpose]
 flour, plus extra for rolling out
100g [¾ cup] white spelt flour
125g [½ cup plus 1 Tbsp] unsalted
 butter, chilled and diced
1 Tbsp poppy seeds
40g [½ cup] finely grated
 Parmesan
about 3 Tbsp ice-cold water
1 tsp white wine vinegar
1 Tbsp dried breadcrumbs
salt and freshly ground
 black pepper

Tomato topping
500g [1lb 2oz] tomatoes, sliced
1 Tbsp chopped fresh oregano
½ Tbsp milk, for glazing
150g [5¼oz] crumbly goat's cheese
2 Tbsp toasted pine nuts
a small handful of basil leaves

Serves 4

Start by making the poppy-seed and Parmesan pastry. Combine the flours in a large bowl, add the chilled, diced butter and rub in using your fingertips. When the butter is almost incorporated but still with flecks visible, add the poppy seeds and half the Parmesan, season well with salt and black pepper and mix to combine.

Mix the ice-cold water with the vinegar and gradually add to the pastry mixture, cutting through with a palette knife and then using your hands to bring the dough together into a ball. You may need more or less water depending on the brand of flours used and room temperature.

Flatten the dough into a disc, wrap in cling film [plastic wrap] and chill for a couple of hours or until firm.

Preheat the oven to 200°C/400°F/Gas 6 and place a solid baking sheet on the middle shelf to heat up.

Lightly dust the work surface with flour and roll the dough out to a round, about 30cm [12in] in diameter. Slide the pastry onto a sheet of baking parchment on top of another baking sheet. Sprinkle the remaining Parmesan and the breadcrumbs onto the pastry, leaving a 2-cm [¾-in] border all around.

Arrange the tomatoes on top of the cheesy breadcrumbs, sprinkling with chopped oregano as you do so, and seasoning with salt and black pepper. Fold the pastry edges over the tomatoes in attractive folds and brush with a little milk.

Slide the galette off the baking sheet, but still on the paper, directly onto the hot baking sheet in the oven and bake for 15 minutes. Reduce the heat to 180°C/350°F/ Gas 4 and bake for a further 15–20 minutes until the pastry is crisp and golden and the tomatoes have started to caramelize at the edges.

Remove from the oven and leave to cool slightly. Crumble over the goat's cheese, sprinkle over the toasted pine nuts and torn basil leaves, and serve.

CURRIED CHICKEN
& LENTIL PIES

These are my go-to, Friday-night pies – they can be made in advance and pulled from the fridge and baked in about 30 minutes. The filling and pastry should be prepared in advance and chilled prior to assembling. They are nourishing and full of flavour – and only need some green veggies and a good selection of Indian pickles to serve alongside.

You can either use pre-cooked brown lentils, or soak and cook dried lentils, which I prefer because they are cheaper and they have a better flavour. If using dried lentils, you will need 100g [3½oz] brown lentils, soaked overnight in at least twice their volume of cold water, then drained, rinsed and cooked in a large pan of water until tender.

Filling
1 large onion, chopped
1 Tbsp olive oil
1 fat garlic clove, crushed
2 tsp grated fresh ginger
3 Tbsp curry paste
1 tsp black mustard seeds
500g [1lb 2oz] skinless, boneless
    chicken thighs, trimmed and
    cut into 2-cm [¾-in] pieces
250ml [1 cup] chicken stock
150ml [²/₃ cup] coconut milk
2 tsp dried curry leaves
200g [7oz] cooked brown lentils
salt and freshly ground
    black pepper

Pastry
300g [2¼ cups] plain [all-purpose]
    flour, plus extra for rolling out
175g [¾ cup plus 1 tsp] unsalted
    butter, chilled and diced
4 Tbsp ice-cold water
2 tsp cider vinegar or white
    wine vinegar
1 Tbsp milk, for glazing

You will need 4 individual foil pie
    dishes, 13cm [5in] across the
    top and 3cm [1¼in] deep

Makes 4 large individual pies

Prepare the filling the day before you plan on assembling and serving these pies, as the flavour will improve after 24 hours, and needs to be chilled.

Tip the onion into a large, heavy-bottomed saucepan, add the olive oil and cook over a low–medium heat until soft but not coloured. Add the garlic, ginger, curry paste and mustard seeds and cook for a further 1–2 minutes.

Add the chicken to the pan and brown over a medium heat in the spicy onion mixture. Pour in the stock and coconut milk, add the curry leaves, season with salt and black pepper and bring slowly to the boil. Reduce the heat to a gentle simmer, cover and cook for about 40 minutes until the chicken is tender, stirring from time to time. Add the cooked lentils and cook for a further 10 minutes. Remove from the heat, leave to cool, then cover and chill until needed.

To make the pastry, tip the flour into a large bowl. Season with salt and black pepper and add the chilled, diced butter. Using a round-bladed or palette knife, cut the butter into the flour until the butter pieces are half their original size. Switch to using your hands to rub the butter into the flour and, when there are only very small flecks of butter still visible, make a well in the middle of the mixture.

continued »

Add the ice-cold water and vinegar and mix using the knife until the pastry starts to clump together. Gather the dough into a ball and knead gently for 20 seconds until smooth. Flatten the dough into a disc, wrap in cling film [plastic wrap] and chill for a couple of hours.

Dust the work surface with flour and divide the pastry into 4 equal portions. Take the first piece of pastry and cut it into two pieces, one twice as large as the other. Roll the larger piece out into a neat round about 2–3mm [$^1/_{16}$–$^1/_8$in] thick, and use to line the foil pie dish, pressing the pastry evenly to cover the base and sides, with a little extra hanging over the top.

Spoon one-quarter of the chilled filling into the pastry-lined dish, and spread level with the back of a spoon. Roll the smaller piece of pastry into a neat round large enough to generously cover the top of the pie. Brush the edges of the pie with water and lay the disc on top to cover the filling. Pinch the edges to seal and trim off any excess pastry. Repeat with the remaining pastry and filling to make 4 pies. Cover and chill for at least 30 minutes or until ready to cook.

Preheat the oven to 190°C/375°F/Gas 5 and place a solid baking sheet on the middle shelf to heat up.

Brush the tops of the pies with milk, cut a hole in the middle of each with a wooden skewer and bake on the hot baking sheet for about 30 minutes until the filling is piping hot and the pastry golden brown and crisp.

PORK PIES

Why make one when you can make two? The effort involved is marginally more but the rewards plentiful. I think this size of pork pie gives a perfect ratio of filling to pastry and you don't run the risk of drying the meat out. To jelly or not is down to you – it helps keep the meat moist and if you do use a flavoursome stock it will only add to the end result. Perfect for a buffet or picnic – don't skimp on the mustard and pickles.

Filling
750g [1lb 11oz] lean pork shoulder
300g [10½oz] skinless, boneless pork belly
200g [7oz] rindless smoked streaky bacon
100g [3½oz] diced Bramley apple
50g [1¾oz] cooked and peeled chestnuts, chopped
½ Tbsp chopped fresh sage
2 tsp fresh thyme leaves
½ tsp ground mace
½ tsp cayenne pepper
½ tsp mustard powder
2 cooking chorizo
2 garlic cloves, very finely chopped
1 Tbsp chopped flat-leaf parsley
1 tsp finely grated lemon zest
1 tsp fennel seeds
salt and freshly black pepper

Hot-water crust pastry
300g [2¼ cups] plain [all-purpose] flour, plus a little extra
250g [1¾ cups] strong white flour
½ tsp caster [granulated] sugar
150g [⅔ cup] lard, diced
50g [3½ Tbsp] unsalted butter, diced
200ml [generous ¾ cup] water
2 medium eggs, beaten
a pinch of sea salt flakes, crushed

Jelly (optional)
400ml [1⅔ cups] fresh pork or veal stock
1 sheet of leaf gelatine

You will need 2 x 15-cm [6-in] springform cake tins

Makes 2 pies, each serving 6

Start by making the filling. Cut the pork shoulder, belly and bacon into 1-cm [³⁄₈-in] dice and mix well. Place two-thirds of the meat in a food processor and pulse until minced – you may need to do this in batches, depending on the size of your food processor. Mix the chopped and minced meats together then weigh and divide the meat evenly between 2 bowls. Add the apple, chestnuts, sage, thyme, mace, cayenne and mustard powder to one bowl, season really well and mix to combine.

Remove the cooking chorizo from its skin, break the meat into little pieces and add to the second bowl along with the garlic, parsley, lemon zest and fennel seeds. Season well with salt and pepper and mix to combine. Cover both meats with cling film [plastic wrap] and chill until needed.

For the hot-water crust pastry, mix the flours, sugar, salt and black pepper in a large bowl and make a well in the middle. Place the lard, butter and water in a small pan and set over a medium heat. Allow the lard and butter to melt in the water and bring to the boil. Roughly mix three-quarters of the beaten egg into the flour, add the hot-water mixture and, working quickly, mix the dough together until smooth. Cover with a clean tea towel and set aside for 20 minutes until cool enough to handle.

Lightly dust the work surface with flour. Weigh the hot-water crust pastry and divide in half. Cover one piece and set aside. Take the other piece and cut it into a further two pieces, with one piece twice the size of the other.

continued »

continued »

Roll the larger piece out to a thickness of about 5mm [¼in] and use to line one of the cake tins, making sure that the pastry evenly covers the base and sides of the tin with no cracks or holes; it should just overhang the top of the tin.

Carefully pack the apple-seasoned meat into the pastry case, mounding it up slightly in the middle. Roll the remaining pastry into an 18-cm [7-in] circle for the lid. Brush the edges of the pastry with water and lay the lid on top, pressing the edges together to seal. Cut off the excess pastry and decoratively crimp the edges of the pie between your fingers. Roll out the pastry trimmings to make leaves to decorate the top of the pie. Brush the top of the pie with the remaining beaten egg, arrange the leaves on top and brush with egg again. Push a wooden skewer through the pastry lid to make a neat hole in the top of the pie and place on a baking sheet. Make the second pie with the remaining pastry and the chorizo-flavoured filling.

Preheat the oven to 180°C/350°F/Gas 4.

Bake the pies for 30 minutes and then reduce the oven temperature to 160°C/320°F/Gas 3 and continue to cook for a further 1¼ hours, glazing the top of each pie again after 45 minutes. The pies should be a deep golden colour and the filling cooked through after this time.

Remove the pies from the oven and leave to rest for 30 minutes. Meanwhile, if adding jelly, pour the stock into a small pan, bring to the boil and reduce to 250–300ml [1–1¼ cups]. Soak the gelatine leaf in a bowl of cold water for a few minutes, then drain and add the floppy gelatine to the hot stock. Stir to melt and then set aside to cool for 15 minutes. Using a small funnel or plain piping nozzle, pour the warm stock slowly, a little at a time, into each pie through the steam hole in the lid to fill the gaps left by the cooked meat. You may need to gently tilt the pie from side to side to help the stock soak in. Leave to cool and then chill overnight before serving with your choice of condiments. Mustard and pickles would be my number-one choice.

PISSALADIERE

This onion, anchovy and olive tart hails from the South of France where you will find variations in most delis. This version has a pizza-style yeasted dough crust but it can also be made with puff pastry if you so desire. Cut into squares and serve as an apéritif with chilled rosé.

The onions and base can be done the night before. Let the dough prove overnight in the fridge and bring to room temperature before rolling out.

Topping

5 Tbsp fruity olive oil
1kg [2lb 3oz] onions, sliced
1 bay leaf
1 bushy sprig of thyme
3 garlic cloves, crushed
a good pinch of sugar
2 Tbsp sun-dried tomato paste
60g [2oz] anchovies in olive oil, drained weight
24 stoned black olives
3 tsp picked thyme leaves
a pinch of espelette pepper or dried chilli flakes [red pepper flakes]
salt and freshly ground black pepper

Base

125g [1 cup minus 1 Tbsp] plain [all-purpose] flour, plus extra for rolling out
125g [¾ cup plus 2 Tbsp] strong white flour
1 tsp fast-action dried yeast
a good pinch of salt
a pinch of caster [granulated] sugar
1 Tbsp extra virgin olive oil
150ml [⅔ cup] warm water

Serves 6–8

Heat 4 tablespoons of the olive oil in a large sauté pan over a low–medium heat. Add the sliced onions, bay leaf and thyme and cook slowly for about 35–40 minutes until tender, stirring from time to time. Add the garlic and cook for a further 5–10 minutes until the onions are really soft and starting to caramelize at the edges. Remove from the heat, pick out the thyme and bay leaf, season well with salt and black pepper and the sugar, and set aside to cool.

For the base, place both flours in a bowl with the yeast, salt and sugar. Make a well in the centre and add the oil and water. Using a wooden spoon, mix until the dough comes together, adding a little more warm water if needed. Turn onto a lightly floured work surface and knead until smooth. (You can also make the dough in a free-standing mixer with a dough hook.) Shape into a smooth ball, put in the bowl and cover with cling film [plastic wrap]. Prove for 1 hour at room temperature, or overnight in the fridge.

Preheat the oven to 190°C/375°F/Gas 5 and place a solid baking sheet on the middle shelf to heat up. When the dough has doubled in size, dust the surface with flour and roll the dough into a rectangle about 40 x 30cm [16 x 12in], and 4mm [⅛in] thick. Slide onto a baking sheet lined with baking parchment. Spread the tomato paste over the dough, leaving a 1-cm [⅜-in] border around the edge. Arrange the cooled onions evenly on top. Bake on the middle shelf for 10 minutes.

Remove the pissaladière from the oven and arrange the anchovies on top in a criss-cross pattern. Scatter with olives and thyme, season with a pinch of espelette pepper or chilli flakes and bake for 10 minutes until the onions are starting to caramelize at the edges and the base is golden and crisp. Cut into squares and serve warm.

BABY LEEK, SPRING ONION & CHARD TART WITH TALEGGIO

I love this green veggie-laden tart with nuggets of creamy Taleggio cheese and a crunch of toasted hazelnuts. It's an ideal lunch tart cut into slices and served with a crisp salad and an even crisper glass of white wine.

If you fancy changing things around you could add some asparagus spears or sliced baby courgettes to the mix and, so long as the cheese is creamy, it could just as easily be something blue such as gorgonzola.

Pastry
250g [1¾ cups plus 2 Tbsp] plain [all-purpose] flour
a good pinch each of salt and freshly ground black pepper
125g [½ cup plus 1 Tbsp] unsalted butter, chilled and diced
4 Tbsp ice-cold water
1 tsp cider vinegar or white wine vinegar

Topping
150g [5¼oz] baby leeks (about 6)
about 8 spring onions [scallions]
1 Tbsp unsalted butter
100g [3½oz] shredded Swiss chard or spring greens
2 medium eggs
200ml [generous ¾ cup] double [heavy] cream
2 Tbsp freshly grated Parmesan
125g [4½oz] Taleggio, broken into nuggets
3 tsp fresh thyme leaves
50g [¾ cup] blanched hazelnuts, roughly chopped
salt and freshly ground black pepper

You will need a 20 x 30-cm [8 x 12-in] baking tin, 3–4cm [1¼–1½in] deep

Serves 6

Prepare the pastry using the ingredients on this page and following the instructions for the Rosemary and Parmesan Pastry on page 14, leaving out the rosemary and Parmesan additions. Chill for at least 1 hour.

Meanwhile, for the topping, trim the leeks and spring onions and cut them to fit into the baking tin. Bring a pan of salted water to the boil and very lightly blanch the leeks – no longer than 1 minute – then drain and leave to dry on a double thickness of kitchen paper [paper towels]. Melt the butter in a frying pan, add the shredded chard or greens, season and cook over a medium heat until just wilted. Remove from the pan and set aside.

Dust the work surface with flour and roll the pastry out into a neat rectangle at least 4cm [1½in] larger all round than the baking tin. Carefully line the tin with the pastry, pressing it neatly into the corners. Chill the pastry shell on a baking sheet for at least 20 minutes while you preheat the oven to 180°C/350°F/Gas 4.

Prick the base of the pastry with a fork, trim any excess pastry from the top of the tin and line with foil and baking rice. Blind bake the pastry on the middle shelf of the oven for about 20 minutes until starting to turn golden at the edges. Remove the foil and rice and continue to cook for a further 3–4 minutes to dry out the base.

Whisk together the eggs, cream and half of the Parmesan, and season well. Fold in the wilted greens, spoon into the pastry and spread level. Arrange the spring onions and blanched leeks on top and tuck nuggets of Taleggio around. Sprinkle with the remaining Parmesan, the thyme leaves and chopped hazelnuts. Bake on the middle shelf for about 25 minutes until the topping is set and golden.

PHEASANT PASTILLA

Pastilla is a classic Moroccan pie often filled with braised and spiced pigeon, amongst other things. I'm making no claims to authenticity here and have used pheasant in this recipe, as they are cheap and easier to come by.

Traditionally pastilla is dusted with icing sugar and cinnamon just before serving. I find this too sweet for my tastes, but do whatever pleases you. However, I do like to serve it with a herby zhoug sauce, which really is flying in the face of authenticity.

2 oven-ready pheasants
2 onions
4 garlic cloves
1 cinnamon stick
2 bay leaves
500ml [generous 2 cups] chicken stock
500ml [generous 2 cups] water
2 Tbsp olive oil
1 tsp cumin seeds
½ tsp ground coriander
¼ tsp ground allspice
a good pinch of saffron strands
¼ tsp dried chilli flakes [red pepper flakes]
250g [8¾oz] butternut squash, peeled and diced
75g [½ cup] dried apricots, halved
50g [1¾oz] pistachios or almonds, roughly chopped
1½ Tbsp pomegranate molasses or clear honey
1–2 tsp rose harissa, to taste
3 Tbsp chopped flat-leaf parsley
2 Tbsp chopped coriander [cilantro]
75g [⅓ cup] unsalted butter, melted
8–10 sheets of filo [phyllo] pastry
salt and freshly ground black pepper

You will need a 23-cm [9-in] springform cake tin

Serves 6

Place the pheasants in a lidded flameproof casserole in which they will fit snugly. Peel and halve one of the onions and add to the casserole. Lightly bash 2 of the garlic cloves with the back of a knife and add, along with the cinnamon and bay leaves. Pour over the stock and water and set the pan over a medium heat. Bring to the boil, reduce to a simmer, half cover with a lid and cook gently for 35–40 minutes until the pheasant is tender and a leg easily pulls away from the body.

Remove the pheasants from the casserole, leave until cool enough to handle then shred the meat from the breasts and thighs. Discard the skin and bones.

While the pheasant is cooling, return the poaching liquid to the heat, bring to the boil and reduce to 400ml [1⅔ cups], spooning off any scum or fat that rises to the surface.

Slice the remaining onion, tip into another large pan, add the olive oil and cook over a medium heat until the onion is tender and just starting to caramelize at the edges. Crush the 2 remaining garlic cloves and add, with the cumin, ground coriander, allspice, saffron and chilli flakes, and cook for a minute more. Add the diced butternut squash, stir to coat in the onion and spices, cover and cook over a low–medium heat for 3–4 minutes. Add the reduced poaching liquor, bring to the boil, scraping the bottom of the pan with a wooden spoon to loosen any cooked-on spices, half cover the pan and cook at a gentle simmer until the squash is tender and the stock reduced slightly.

continued »

Tip the pheasant meat into the casserole along with the apricots, pistachios, molasses and harissa. Mix well to combine – there should be enough liquid to unctuously coat the pheasant. Taste, season with salt and black pepper, and more harissa if needed. Add the chopped herbs and leave to cool.

Preheat the oven to 180°C/350°F/Gas 4.

Brush one sheet of filo with melted butter and lay it in the cake tin to cover the base and sides, allowing any excess to hang over the top. Filo sheets vary in size from brand to brand so you'll have to use your judgement here but you'll need enough excess hanging over the edge to half cover the top of the pie to finish. Brush another pastry sheet with butter and lay in the tin at an angle to the first, and covering the base and side. Repeat layering with buttered filo to completely cover the base and sides of the tin.

Spoon the pheasant mixture into the pastry-lined tin and spread level. Fold the excess pastry back over the top of the pheasant in generous pleats or ruffles. Brush over any remaining butter and place the tin on a baking sheet. Bake on the middle shelf of the oven for 30 minutes until the pastry is crisp and golden and the filling is piping hot.

Leave the pastilla to rest in the tin for about 2–3 minutes then transfer to a serving plate. Cut into wedges to serve.

BRUNCH PIE

My friend Harry likens people to food; we have a friend who is cake sprinkles and another who is grilled cheese sandwiches. If my boyfriend were a food he'd be this pie. This is essentially a good old fried breakfast – in a pie. But not an ordinary pie – the crust is rosti potatoes rather than pastry, which pleases him greatly.

A hunk of bread is ideal for mopping up the egg in the bottom of the pan.

2 Tbsp olive oil
8 slices of smoked streaky bacon
8 chestnut mushrooms, quartered
  or halved, depending on size
750g [1lb 11oz] red-skinned
  potatoes (such as Desiree)
1 tsp smoked paprika
1 tsp garlic granules
25g [1¾ Tbsp] unsalted butter
50g [3½oz] Gruyère, Fontina or
  Cheddar, grated
150ml [²/₃ cup] double
  [heavy] cream
12 cherry tomatoes
4 medium eggs
140g [5oz] chorizo, sliced
2 tsp thyme leaves
salt and freshly ground
  black pepper

You will need a 20-cm [8-in]
  ovenproof frying pan or
  cast-iron skillet

Serves 4

Preheat the oven to 180°C/350°F/Gas 4.

Heat 1 tablespoon of the olive oil in the ovenproof frying pan or skillet. Add the bacon and cook over a medium–high heat just until the fat starts to crisp. Remove from the pan and set aside. Add the mushrooms to the pan and cook quickly in the residual bacon fat until just browned and softened. Remove from the pan, add to the bacon and wipe out any excess oil from the pan.

Peel and coarsely grate the potatoes, tip onto a clean tea towel, gather the ends of the cloth together and squeeze the excess moisture from the potatoes. Scoop into a bowl, add the remaining olive oil, the smoked paprika and garlic granules, and season with salt and black pepper.

Spread the butter onto the bottom and sides of the pan or skillet, to coat evenly. Tip the grated potatoes into the pan and press to cover the base and sides in an even thickness. Set the pan over a low–medium heat for 5 minutes to soften the potatoes on the base of the pan, then slide the pan into the preheated oven and cook for 20–25 minutes until the potatoes have dried out, become pale golden and crisped around the edges.

Sprinkle the grated cheese into the pan and pour over the cream. Arrange the mushrooms, bacon and cherry tomatoes on top. Crack the eggs into the pan – positioning one in each quarter of the pan – and arrange the sliced chorizo around. Sprinkle the thyme leaves on top, season with black pepper and return the pan to the oven for a further 10–12 minutes until the eggs are set and cooked but the yolks still runny. Serve immediately, either cut into portions, allowing one egg per person, or stick the pan in the middle of the table and allow everyone to tuck in.

PIZZA PIE

This recipe is loosely based on Sicilian *impanata* – a yeasted dough, double crusted and filled with cheese, greens and other delicious things. I have filled this version with my favourite pizza toppings – slightly bitter greens, Italian fennel sausage and cheese, cheese and more cheese – and a hit of chilli for good measure.

Good-quality, flavoursome, meaty sausages are vital here – look in your local Italian deli as most will stock a fennel, chilli or perhaps rosemary sausage. The greens are adaptable and although I suggest cavolo nero, which is widely available, I have also made this successfully using broccoli rabe, broccoli spigarello or kale.

You can also swap the sausages for anchovies, add some artichoke hearts, roasted peppers, capers, olives… You could even try breaking an egg into the middle of the greens.

Dough
200g [1½ cups minus 1 Tbsp] strong white flour, plus extra for rolling out
200g [1½ cups] '00' flour
5g [scant ¼oz] fast-action dried yeast
1 tsp caster [granulated] sugar
1 tsp salt
2 Tbsp extra virgin olive oil
about 250ml [1 cup] tepid water

Filling
350g [¾lb] fennel seed or rosemary Italian sausages
1 Tbsp olive oil
150g [5¼oz] trimmed cavolo nero, cut into large pieces
1 fat garlic clove, crushed
a good pinch of dried chilli flakes [red pepper flakes]
100g [3½oz] buffalo mozzarella, torn into pieces
100g [3½oz] Taleggio cheese, torn into pieces
2 Tbsp grated pecorino
1–2 tsp peperoncino paste (optional)
salt and freshly ground black pepper

Serves 3–4

For the dough, tip the flours into a large bowl, add the yeast, sugar and salt and mix well to combine. Make a well in the middle, add the olive oil and water and mix well again to combine, adding more water if the mixture looks too dry – it needs to be soft and quite sticky. Knead until smooth, either by hand or in a free-standing mixer and using a dough hook.

Shape the dough into a ball and place in a large oiled bowl, cover loosely with cling film [plastic wrap] and leave to prove at room temperature for about 1 hour or until doubled in size.

Remove the sausages from their casings and tear the meat into walnut-sized nuggets. Heat the oil in a large frying pan over a high heat, add the sausage pieces and cook quickly to brown. Remove from the pan with a slotted spoon and set aside.

Add the cavolo nero to the frying pan with the garlic and chilli flakes, season with salt and black pepper and cook quickly until wilted. Remove from the pan and set aside.

SAVOURY

206

continued »

Preheat the oven to 200°C/400°F/Gas 6 and place a solid baking sheet on the middle shelf to heat up at the same time.

Dust the work surface with flour, turn the dough out of the bowl and divide in half. Roll one piece of dough out into a large round, about 30cm [12in] in diameter. Take your time as the dough will want to spring back into a smaller shape. Slide onto a baking sheet lined with baking parchment and top with the cavolo nero, leaving a 1–2-cm [3/8–3/4-in] border all around the edge. Add the sausage then the mozzarella and Taleggio. Sprinkle the pecorino over the top and drizzle with peperoncino paste, if using.

Brush the border with water. Roll out the second piece of dough on the floured work surface into a round of roughly the same shape and size as the first piece. This bit is tricky: working quickly, dust the top of the dough with a little flour to stop it sticking, fold it in half and carefully lift the dough up and lay it on top of the pizza to cover one half. Unfold the dough to cover the entire pizza, press the edges together to seal and crimp between your fingers.

Slide the pizza pie, still on its parchment, onto the hot baking sheet in the oven and cook for about 30 minutes until risen, golden brown and the filling is bubbling and piping hot. Serve hot, at room temperature or cold, cut into big wedges.

ROASTED PEPPER, SLUMPED TOMATO & WHIPPED FETA TART

This tart is like a ray of sunshine and ideal for serving at your next al fresco summer lunch. Roast the tomatoes and peppers in advance and you'll be ready for a swift assembly in moments.

You could cut multiple corners here – use storebought puff pastry (always, always all-butter) and a jar of roasted peppers and sun-dried or sun-blush tomatoes (but it won't be the same, of course). In fact, I'd be inclined to make up double the amount of tomatoes – they'll keep for a week in the fridge and will liven up most salads or avo on toast.

200g [7oz] cherry tomatoes
3 garlic cloves
1 sprig of rosemary
1 sprig of basil
4 Tbsp extra virgin olive oil
2 red and 2 yellow [bell] peppers
2 Tbsp olive oil
375g [13¼oz] all–butter puff
   pastry (see page 12 for
   homemade and use ½ quantity)
plain [all-purpose] flour,
   for rolling out
200g [7oz] feta cheese
50g[1¾oz] toasted and salted
   or smoked almonds, roughly
   chopped
a handful baby leaf purple basil
   or other micro herbs
salt and freshly ground
   black pepper

Serves 4–6

Start by making the slumped tomatoes, which can be prepared a few days in advance and stored in the fridge until ready to use.

Preheat the oven to 150°C/300°F/Gas 2. Cut the tomatoes in half horizontally, tip into a small roasting tray in which they will fit in a snug single layer and arrange cut side up. Lightly bash the garlic cloves with the flat side of your knife – just to break the skin – and tuck in with the tomatoes. Nestle the sprigs of rosemary and basil among the tomatoes, season with salt and black pepper and spoon over the extra virgin olive oil. Slow-roast in the oven for 1¼ hours – maybe 15 minutes longer – until they are tender and the edges are only just starting to colour. Leave to cool then cover and chill until needed.

Turn the oven up to 200°C/400°F/Gas 6.

Cut the peppers in half, remove the stalks and shake out the seeds. Place the peppers cut side down on a large baking sheet, drizzle with the oil and roast for 20–25 minutes until the skin is charred and blistered. Leave to cool and then peel off the skin.

Roll the pastry out on a floured work surface to a neat rectangle about 20 x 35cm [8 x 14in], trim the edges to

continued »

continued »

neaten and slide onto a baking sheet lined
with baking parchment. Prick the pastry all
over with a fork and pop into the fridge to
chill for 20 minutes.

Lay a sheet of parchment on top of the
pastry and place another baking sheet
on top – this will stop it rising unevenly
as it cooks. Bake the pastry on the middle
shelf of the oven for 20 minutes until
puffed and golden, then remove the
sheet and parchment and cook for another
5 minutes to crisp up. Leave to cool to
room temperature.

Crumble the feta into a mini whizzer or
food processor, squeeze in the tomatoey
roasted garlic from their skins, add
3 tablespoons of the roast tomato oil from
the tray, season with black pepper and
blend until smooth and creamy. Spread
the whipped feta mixture onto the pastry,
leaving a little border all around.

Cut the peppers into strips, lay them
on top of the feta layer and arrange the
slumped tomatoes around. Scatter the
chopped almonds on top, garnish with
herbs, drizzle with any leftover tomato oil
and serve immediately.

CHARD & FETA PIE

This pie should be eaten soon after baking to fully enjoy and appreciate the contrast between the super crispy pastry and hot veggie filling laced with nuggets of salty, creamy feta.

1 large onion, sliced
1 large fennel bulb, trimmed
  and sliced
3 Tbsp olive oil
2 fat garlic cloves, chopped
300g [10½oz] Swiss chard, washed
1 rounded Tbsp chopped parsley
1 rounded Tbsp chopped dill
1 tsp finely grated lemon zest
1 large courgette [zucchini]
50g [3½ Tbsp] unsalted butter,
  melted
250g [8¾oz] (8 sheets) filo
  [phyllo] pastry
150g [5¼oz] feta cheese
3 medium eggs
2 tsp sesame seeds
salt and freshly ground
  black pepper

You will need a 20 x 30-cm
[8 x 12-in] rectangular
baking tin

Serves 4–6

Cook the sliced onion and fennel gently in a large sauté pan in 2 tablespoons of the olive oil until really soft but not coloured. Add the chopped garlic and cook for a further 30 seconds. Cut the chard stalks into 1-cm [3/8-in] thick slices, add to the pan and cook until softened.

Meanwhile, cut the chard leaves into 1–2-cm [3/8–3/4-in] thick strips. Add to the pan, season well and cook until wilted. Remove from the heat, add the chopped herbs and lemon zest and mix well.

Slice the courgette into rounds no thicker than 3mm [1/8in] and sauté quickly in the remaining olive oil until just tender. Season and remove from the pan.

Preheat the oven to 180°C/350°F/Gas 4.

Brush the baking tin with melted butter and lay one sheet of filo in the bottom, allowing the pastry to hang over the sides. Brush with melted butter and top with another sheet of filo. Repeat this layering until you have 4 layers of pastry, each brushed with butter. Spoon the chard mixture into the tin and spread level. Crumble over the feta and arrange the courgette slices on top. Beat the eggs together and season well. Pour the eggs over the top of the veggies, allowing them to seep through.

Brush the remaining pastry sheets with more butter, lightly scrunch them into crumpled handkerchief shapes and arrange on top of the pie. Sprinkle with sesame seeds and bake on the middle shelf of the oven for about 25 minutes until the filling is hot and the pastry is crisp and golden. Serve hot or warm.

POTATO, ONION & CHEESE TART

I wrote this recipe on a particularly bleak winter's day when I was clearly craving carbs and melted cheese. This is restorative tucker for when you've been toiling away outdoors in the cold or want to imagine yourself dining in an Alpine restaurant with snow falling outside.

Try adding either anchovies or air-dried ham such as prosciutto, tucked in amongst the potatoes.

Rosemary & Parmesan pastry

250g [1¾ cups plus 2 Tbsp] plain [all-purpose] flour, plus extra for rolling out

a good pinch each of salt and freshly ground black pepper

125g [½ cup plus 1 Tbsp] unsalted butter, chilled and diced

50g [¾ cup] freshly grated Parmesan

1 Tbsp finely chopped rosemary

about 4 Tbsp ice-cold water

1 tsp cider vinegar or white wine vinegar

Filling

700g [1lb 9oz] red-skinned waxy potatoes such as Roseval

2 onions, sliced

20g [1½ Tbsp] unsalted butter

1 Tbsp olive oil

300ml [1¼ cups] double [heavy] cream

1 medium egg plus 1 medium yolk

2 garlic cloves, crushed

100g [1⅓ cups] grated Gruyère

1 large sprig of rosemary, leaves roughly chopped

salt and freshly ground black pepper

You will need a 20 x 30-cm [8 x 12-in] rectangular baking tin

Serves 8

Prepare the rosemary and Parmesan pastry following the instructions on page 14. Chill for at least 1 hour.

Parboil the whole, unpeeled potatoes in salted water for 10 minutes until just tender. Drain, cool and thinly slice.

While the potatoes are cooking, tip the onions into a frying pan with the butter and olive oil, season and cook over a medium heat until soft and starting to caramelize at the edges. Leave to cool.

Roll out the pastry on a lightly floured surface to a rectangle about 40 x 30cm [16 x 12in], and use to line the brownie or baking tin. Trim the excess from the top, crimp the edges and chill for 30 minutes.

Preheat the oven to 190°C/375°F/Gas 5 and place a solid baking sheet on the middle shelf to heat up.

Prick the base of the pastry shell with a fork, line with foil, fill with baking rice and blind bake on the hot baking sheet for 20 minutes until golden at the edges. Remove the foil and rice and continue to bake for a further 3–4 minutes to dry out the base.

Whisk together the cream, egg, extra yolk and the garlic, and season well. Scatter the cooled onions over the pastry base and top with half of the grated Gruyère. Pour over the egg mixture and fan the potato slices on top, then sprinkle with the remaining cheese and the rosemary. Place on the hot baking sheet and bake in the oven for 35 minutes until the pastry is crisp and the potatoes and filling are golden.

Cool for a few moments then serve hot, warm or at room temperature, cut into squares.

TARTE FLAMBÉE

This is not a tarte flambée in its truest form, which is traditionally topped with fromage blanc or crème fraîche, sliced onions and smoked bacon lardons and perhaps some Munster cheese; this is my springtime twist. The basic elements are here – a crisp pizza-like base, a creamy topping and sliced onions. But this is where the similarities end – I have swapped out the bacon for asparagus, broccoli and peas. Once cooked, it's topped with sprightly pea shoots, a crumble of feta and a scattering of herbs.

Dough
100g [¾ cup] strong white flour
100g [¾ cup] '00' flour
1 tsp fast-action dried yeast
a good pinch of caster
  [granulated] sugar
a good pinch of salt
1 Tbsp extra virgin olive oil
125ml [½ cup] warm water

Topping
200g [scant 1 cup] full-fat cream
  cheese, fromage blanc or
  crème fraîche
1 Tbsp snipped chives
  (or chopped wild garlic
  leaves if in season)
75 [⅔ cup] peas (defrosted
  if frozen)
200g [7oz] Tenderstem broccoli
8 asparagus spears
1 banana [echalion] shallot
  or small white onion, very
  thinly sliced
1 Tbsp extra virgin olive oil
a handful of pea shoots
100g [7oz] crumbled feta
  or ricotta salata
a small bunch of dill,
  very roughly chopped
salt and freshly ground
  black pepper

Serves 4–6

Start by making the dough. Tip both of the flours into a large bowl, add the yeast, sugar and salt and mix well to combine. Make a well in the middle, add the olive oil and water and mix well to combine, adding a drop more water if the mixture looks too dry – it needs to be soft and just a little sticky. Tip the dough onto a surface and knead for 5 minutes until smooth and elastic – as this is a small quantity of dough it's not really worth using a mixer. Shape the dough into a ball, place in a large oiled bowl, cover with cling film [plastic wrap] and leave to prove at room temperature for 1 hour or until doubled in size.

While the dough is proving, prepare the topping. Spoon the cream cheese into a bowl, add the snipped chives and season with black pepper. If using fresh peas, blanch in boiling water for 1 minute then refresh under cold water. Trim the broccoli and asparagus and slice them in half.

Preheat the oven to 200°C/400°F/Gas 6.

Dust the work surface with flour, turn the dough out of the bowl and lightly knead to knock out any air bubbles. Slowly roll the dough into a thin circle, roughly 30cm [12in] in diameter (if you do this too quickly the dough will simply shrink back into a small circle), and place on a parchment-lined or lightly floured baking sheet. Spread the herby cream cheese over the dough, leaving a 1-cm [³⁄₈-in] border all around. Scatter with the sliced shallot and peas and top with the broccoli and asparagus. Season with salt and black pepper and drizzle with the extra virgin olive oil. Bake on the middle shelf for about 15 minutes until the base is puffed, golden brown and crisp.

Leave to cool for 2–3 minutes and then scatter over the pea shoots, crumbled feta and dill. Serve cut into wedges.

LOBSTER PIE FOR TWO

A date-night dinner. You'll find cooked lobster meat at most good fishmongers, though you may need to order it in advance. Failing that, cooked whole lobsters are available in larger supermarkets – either fresh or frozen. You will need two small whole lobsters or one large one to yield this quantity of meat. If you do use whole lobsters, don't waste the shells – use them to make extra shellfish stock for another time.

100g [3½oz] all-butter puff pastry
(see page 12 for homemade)
plain [all-purpose] flour,
for rolling out
1 egg, beaten, to glaze

Filling
25g [2 Tbsp] unsalted butter
15g [1¾ Tbsp] plain [all-purpose]
flour
200ml [generous ¾ cup]
shellfish stock
1 Tbsp brandy
1 medium egg yolk
2 Tbsp double [heavy] cream
1 tsp Dijon mustard
a good pinch of cayenne pepper
1 Tbsp snipped chives
½ Tbsp chopped tarragon
25g [⅓ cup] freshly grated
Parmesan
225–250g [8–9oz] cooked lobster
meat, cut into bite-sized pieces
salt and freshly ground
black pepper

You will need 2 small, shallow
ovenproof dishes

Serves 2

Start by making the filling. Melt the butter in a small saucepan, add the flour and cook for 30 seconds, stirring constantly until it starts to smell biscuity. Gradually add the stock, still on the heat and stirring constantly until the sauce is smooth and thickened. Bring to the boil and simmer gently for 3 minutes. Add the brandy, egg yolk, cream, mustard and cayenne and cook for a further 30 seconds until smooth. Add the chopped herbs and grated Parmesan, mix well to combine, season with salt and black pepper and remove from the heat.

Divide the lobster between the two ovenproof dishes, pour over the sauce to cover, and leave to cool.

Dust the work surface with flour and divide the puff pastry into two pieces. Roll out the pastry to a thickness of about 2mm [1/16in] and into a shape 2–3cm [1/16–1/8in] larger than the top of your dishes. Trim the edges to neaten, brush the top of the dishes with a little water and place the pastry on top, pressing the edges to seal. Brush the pastry with beaten egg and chill while you preheat the oven to 190°C/375°F/Gas 5.

Cut a small steam hole in the top of each pie, place on a baking sheet and cook on the middle shelf of the oven for about 25 minutes until the pastry is crisp, puffed and golden brown and the filling is piping hot.

Serve with new potatoes and buttery spinach or some steamed asparagus.

SMOKED HADDOCK & CELERIAC PIE

Sweet braised celeriac is a wonderful contrast to salty smoked haddock, and when topped with buttery puff pastry this makes a most pleasing and delicious pie.

As always I prefer to make my own puff pastry but do appreciate that it's not everyone's favourite pastime. If you are using storebought, do make sure that it is the all-butter variety.

75g [⅓ cup] unsalted butter
600g [1lb 5oz] celeriac [celery root] (roughly ½ large celeriac), peeled and cut into 2-cm [¾-in] dice
a bushy sprig of thyme
125ml [½ cup] vegetable stock
500g [1lb 2oz] undyed, skinless, boneless smoked haddock
500ml [generous 2 cups] whole milk
2 bay leaves
6 spring onions [scallions], cut into 2-cm [¾-in] lengths
2 Tbsp plain [all-purpose] flour, plus extra for rolling out
1 Tbsp Dijon mustard
a good grating of nutmeg
1 rounded Tbsp chopped parsley
1 heaped Tbsp capers, drained
370g [13oz] all-butter puff pastry (see page 12 for homemade, and use ½ quantity)
1 egg, beaten, for glazing
salt and freshly ground black pepper

You will need an ovenproof gratin dish

Serves 4

Preheat the oven to 180°C/350°F/Gas 4.

Melt a third of the butter in a heavy-based ovenproof frying pan over a medium heat. Add the celeriac, season with salt and black pepper and cook, stirring often, until starting to turn golden on all sides. Tuck in the thyme sprig with the celeriac, pour over the stock, cover with foil and braise on the middle shelf of the oven for 10–15 minutes until tender and the stock has been absorbed.

Remove the celeriac from the pan and set aside. Cut the smoked haddock into large pieces that will fit into the pan in a single layer. Pour over half of the milk, tuck in the bay leaves, cover with foil and poach in the oven for about 20 minutes until the fish is cooked through. Using a fish slice, remove the haddock from the pan and set aside, reserving the poaching milk for the sauce.

Melt the remaining butter in a medium saucepan, add the spring onions and cook quickly until softened. Remove from the pan with a slotted spoon and set aside with the celeriac and haddock. Add the flour to the butter in the pan and cook, stirring constantly until the mixture starts to smell toasted and biscuity. Strain the haddock poaching milk into the pan and whisk to combine over a low–medium heat. Bring to the boil, gradually add the remaining milk, whisking until smooth, and cook at a very gentle simmer for about 7 minutes until thickened and smooth. Add the mustard and nutmeg and check the seasoning (remembering that the smoked haddock may be salty and you most likely will not need to add more).

continued »

Break the poached haddock into large flakes and arrange in the ovenproof gratin dish with the celeriac and spring onions. Scatter over the parsley and capers and pour over the sauce. Leave to cool and then cover until ready to top with pastry.

Dust the work surface with flour and roll out the pastry into a similar shape to the top of your dish, allowing an extra 2cm [¾in] all round. Brush the edges of the dish with a little water and cover the pie with the pastry. Crimp or pleat the edges and cut a steam hole in the top of the pastry. Any off-cuts can be re-rolled, cut into fish or leaf shapes and stuck on top of the pie with a little water. Brush the pastry with beaten egg and chill for 30 minutes while you preheat the oven to 190°C/375°F/Gas 5.

Cook the pie on a solid baking sheet in the middle of the oven for about 40 minutes until the pastry is crisp and golden and the filling bubbling and piping hot. You may need to add another 5 minutes of cooking time if the pie has been assembled and chilled for more than 1 hour.

Serve with some steamed peas or greens.

PUMPKIN, CAVOLO NERO & GORGONZOLA TART

Here's a deeply savoury tart filled with caramelized roasted pumpkin,
bitter greens, salty blue cheese, squidges of roast garlic and hits of warm
espelette pepper. You've got yourself a tasty lunch. If you can't get hold
of espelette pepper you could use dried chilli flakes, a pinch of smoked
paprika or a drizzle of harissa.

Parmesan pastry
250g [1 cup plus 2 Tbsp] plain
  [all-purpose] flour, plus extra
  for rolling out
a good pinch each of salt and
  freshly ground black pepper
125g [½ cup plus 1 Tbsp] unsalted
  butter, chilled and diced
50g [¾ cup] finely grated
  Parmesan
about 4 Tbsp ice-cold water
1 tsp cider vinegar or white
  wine vinegar

Filling
700g [1lb9oz] pumpkin, peeled
  weight (queen or butternut
  squash are ideal)
2 Tbsp olive oil
4 fat garlic cloves
100g [3½oz] cavolo nero, trimmed
4 medium eggs
350g [1½ cups] ricotta
50g [²/₃ cup] grated Parmesan
  or pecorino,
100g [3½oz] gorgonzola, broken
  into pieces
1 Tbsp pumpkin seeds
a good pinch of espelette pepper
salt and freshly ground
  black pepper

You will need a 25-cm [10-in]
  tart tin or ring

Serves 6–8

Prepare the Parmesan pastry using the ingredients on this
page and following the instructions on page 14 (leaving
out the rosemary addition). Chill for at least 2 hours.

Meanwhile, preheat the oven to 190°C/375°F/Gas 5. Cut
the peeled pumpkin into thick slices, tip into a roasting
tray, toss with the olive oil and season well with salt and
black pepper. Add the whole, unpeeled garlic cloves, mix
to combine and roast on the middle shelf of the oven
for about 30 minutes until tender and just starting to
caramelize at the edges. Leave to cool.

Blanch the cavolo nero leaves in boiling, salted water
for 30 seconds to soften. Drain, cool under cold running
water and pat dry on kitchen paper [paper towels].

Dust the work surface with flour and roll out the pastry to
a neat round, 5cm [2in] larger all round than the tart tin.
Carefully line the tin, pressing the pastry into the corners,
leaving the excess pastry hanging over the edges, and chill
for 20 minutes while you continue to prepare the filling.
Place a solid baking sheet on the middle shelf of the oven
to heat up.

Whisk together the eggs, ricotta and Parmesan. Season
well with salt and black pepper and pour the mixture into
the pastry case. Arrange the roasted pumpkin wedges and
cavolo nero on top, squeeze the soft roasted garlic from
its skin and dot the garlic purée around the veggies along
with the gorgonzola. Sprinkle with the pumpkin seeds
and espelette pepper, slide the tart onto the hot baking
sheet and cook for 30–35 minutes until the pastry is crisp
and the filling is set and golden. Using a serrated knife,
trim the excess pastry from the top of the tart and serve
hot, warm or at room temperature, cut into wedges.

INDEX

Publishing Director: Sarah Lavelle
Comissioning Editor: Céline Hughes
Design and Art Direction: Gemma Hayden
Food Stylist: Annie Rigg
Photographer: Nassima Rothacker
Prop Stylist: Tabitha Hawkins
Food Stylist Assistants: Lola Milne and India Whiley-Morton
Production Controller: Tom Moore
Production Director: Vincent Smith

Published in 2018 by Quadrille, an imprint of Hardie Grant Publishing

Quadrille
52–54 Southwark Street
London SE1 1UN
quadrille.com

Cataloguing in Publication Data: a catalogue record for this book is available from the British Library.

Text © Annie Rigg 2018
Photography © Nassima Rothacker 2018
Design and layout © Quadrille Publishing Limited 2018

ISBN: 978 1 78713 187 3

Printed in China

ACKNOWLEDGEMENTS

This book is dedicated to my step-father Roberto, who is everything.

Without wanting this to sound like an Oscar winner's speech… writing this book has been an utter joy and I have been blessed with a team of brilliant, brilliant folk who have taken my words on a screen and created these pages.

My wonderful publisher Quadrille – thank you for taking on this pastry-laden project and me. My editor Céline Hughes – whom I first had the pleasure of working with about 12 years ago and who is the lady with her hands firmly on the steering wheel on this book. With your patience, kindness, wisdom and gentle manner you are a joy to work with again. Gemma Hayden, an epic designer of dreams – who just got it and combined my words and Nassima's pictures to make this book so smashing. And the team who I never get to meet but without whom this book just wouldn't have come together: Sally Somers on copy-editing duty – thank you for being so diligent; proofreader Sarah Epton – thank you for your eagle-eyed double and triple checking; and a huge thank you to Tom Moore in Production for all the finer details.

One of the many joys in my working life is that I get to work with some super-duper creative talents who over the years have become great friends. Tabitha Hawkins is not only one of the best prop stylists around, she's a creative force who brings so much more than pretty plates to every assignment and despite her best efforts has yet to persuade me to take a Zumba class.

Photographer Nassima Rothacker – for whom nothing is too much trouble, who never stops smiling and whose incredibly beautiful pictures grace these pages. Nassima and Tabitha are two of the most life-affirming chicks you're ever likely to meet and working with them both was a dream. And Nassima's wonderful assistant, Maria, for her hand modelling as well as her help on the shoots.

Lola and India, my long-suffering and fabulous assistants – thank you for sticking with me for another book shoot and keeping the pastry madness rolling…

Over the months of writing and testing this book an awful lot of pies were made and eaten. Thank you to The Hawes for tasting almost every recipe in this book. It's a tough job but someone's got to do it.

And my home team… Hughie – who came up with the initial idea for this book (although the kebabs element didn't make the cut) and never moaned when he had to eat pastry-based breakfasts, lunches and dinners day after day. You are my voice of reason, biggest supporter and love of my life. And the two other 'people' who deserve a mention, Percy and Nellie – my adorable pie-thieving dogs who can scoff a freshly baked and cooling pie in the blink of an eye. I'd like to think that they have discerning palates, but they're just chancers.